Write from the Heart
Grammar Practice

A Companion Exercise Book to

Write from the Heart: A Resource Guide to Engage Writers

By Veldorah J. Rice

www.WriteFromTheHeart.org

Copyright page

Write from the Heart: A Resource Guide to Engage Writers by Veldorah J. Rice Published by Write from the Heart PO Box 1451 Indiana, Pa 15701

www.WriteFromTheHeart.org

For additional resources, go to: www.writefromtheheart.org/resourceguide

For permissions contact: inquiry@writefromtheheart.org

For information about special discounts available for bulk purchases, sales promotions, fund-raising and educational needs, contact Write from the Heart at inquiry@writefromtheheart.org.

Cover by Carrie Scrufari.

All student examples used by permission.

Printed in the United States of America

First Edition

ISBN: 978-1-7353465-2-6 (paperback)

ISBN: 978-1-7353465-3-3 (ebook)

Table of Contents

How to Use This Book

Write from the Heart's Grammar Practice is intended to be used in conjunction with *Write from the Heart: A Resource Guide to Engage Writers.* Each unit of exercises found here correspond to the chapters found in Section 9 of the Resource Guide.

Students can complete each unit after reading the chapters in the Resource Guide, or they can be completed as standalone exercises. The units are set up to move through the basics of parts of speech into building sentences and finally correcting errors within a finished essay.

Every chapter includes individual worksheets for every skill covered and culminates with a unit test that requires students to create their own sentences using the grammar skills covered in that section. Additional Improvement Practice includes holistic grammar exercises that combine all units of study.

Write from the Heart's online classes includes grammar exercises within its full credit classes, and focuses practical grammar training within the writing process. These exercises could be used as extra practice by students taking the online program, as the assignments are unique to this workbook.

For additional resources, including teacher support and student examples, go to www.writefromtheheart.org/resourceguide.

About Write from the Heart

Write from the Heart is an online writing and literature program designed for middle and high school students. We believe that every child should not only be able to read and write but should be able to do both in a way that displays their uniqueness. No child is the same, and each one has a distinct perspective on the world. However, expressing that perspective in written form can sometimes be difficult—for some children, there is a disconnect between what is in their heads and what ends up on the page. We desire to bridge that gap and give every child the tools to more closely connect voice, ideas, and writing.

Write from the Heart offers full credit composition and literature classes for homeschooled middle and high school students, including an accredited AP® English course. We also offer 4-week skills workshops for students in any learning environment, as well as individualized coaching for students through college.

Founded in 2005, Write from the Heart has served families all over the world. Our students are recognized in publications and contests every year, and several have won college scholarships for works they completed through our classes.

Our offerings can be found at www.writefromtheheart.org.

Special Thanks

Special thanks to James Hahn for all his hard work in creating many of these exercises. Getting to know him as a budding student writer during his time at Write from the Heart was a joy, and being able to work with him professionally has been delightful.

Unit 1: Parts of Speech

All the exercises in this unit correspond to the Parts of Speech chapter in *Write from the Heart: A Resource Guide to Engage Writers.*

Students can read each subsection of the chapter and complete the worksheets as follows:

Parts of Speech Subsection	Worksheets Available
Nouns	Worksheet 1.1: Common Nouns vs. Proper Nouns Worksheet 1.2: Concrete Nouns vs. Abstract Nouns Worksheet 1.3: Singular vs. Plural vs. Mass Nouns Worksheet 1.4: Uses of Nouns
Pronouns	Worksheet 1.5: Pronouns and Antecedents Worksheet 1.6: Pronouns and Person ** Worksheet 1.7: Reflexive and Indefinite Pronouns Worksheet 1.8: Relative and Interrogative Pronouns
Verbs	Worksheet 1.9: Verb Expressions Worksheet 1.10: Transitive and Intransitive Verbs Worksheet 1.11: Active and Passive Verbs Worksheet 1.12: Verb Tense
Adjectives and Adverbs	Worksheet 1.13: Adjectives and Adverbs Worksheet 1.14: What Adverbs Modify Worksheet 1.15: Articles
Prepositions and Prepositional Phrases	Worksheet 1.16: Prepositional Phrases
Conjunctions	Worksheet 1.17: Conjunctions
Interjections and Appositives	Worksheet 1.18: Interjections and Appositives
Summary of Unit	Unit 1 Test

Name:_____   Date: _____

Grade: _____

Instructions: Circle the common nouns and underline the proper nouns in each sentence below.

1. I want to travel to many different countries, but especially France.

2. Chloe attended Stanford University for her college degree.

3. Sam's favorite season is summer, but she was born in January.

4. Terry's favorite place to go for a special treat is McDonald's.

5. My brother's favorite holiday is Easter, but my favorite holiday is the Fourth of July.

6. Sometimes, communication in my family is confusing, because my mom's name is Joan, and my aunt's name is Jean.

7. One of my favorite things to do in my spare time is to play Mario Kart.

8. Someday, our family would like to visit New York City to see the Empire State Building and the Statue of Liberty.

9. What Grandma said at dinner made the whole family very emotional.

10. We are going to see the fireworks that John is setting off.

Score: _____

Worksheet 1.2: Concrete Nouns vs. Abstract Nouns

Instructions: In the following sentences, circle the abstract nouns and underline the concrete nouns. Make sure to label all the nouns.

1. Abraham Lincoln is famously remembered as never being able to tell a lie.

2. The eagle in the United States represents freedom.

3. Owls are often portrayed in stories, movies, and cartoons as being smart.

4. Gifts are wonderful, but kindness means more to me.

5. My little brother was in pain, but the BandAid made him feel better.

6. How the cat learned to operate the icemaker is still a mystery to me.

7. We love where we vacation each summer because it is so beautiful.

8. I don't know why the song brings me such joy, but I can't stop listening to it.

9. Whoever ate the last piece of cake probably has chocolate lips that will reveal the truth.

10. My parents can be strict, but I know it is out of love.

Score: _____

Name:_____ Date: _____

Grade: _____

Worksheet 1.3: Singular vs. Plural vs. Mass Nouns

Instructions: Indicate whether the highlighted nouns in the sentences below are singular, plural, or mass.

1. **Money** isn't everything.

2. The **teacher** instructed the **students**.

3. They asked the **family** about all their **trips**.

4. The **cars** all rolled to a stop.

5. The **child** hugged her **mother**.

6. **Happiness** is fleeting, but never gone forever.

7. **Women** make up slightly more than half of the U.S. **population.**

8. **Time** heals most **wounds**.

Score: _____

Worksheet 1.4: Uses of Nouns

Instructions: Identify the use of the bolded nouns in the sentences below—either subject, object, predicate, or possessive.

1. The **mom** called her **son** to the kitchen.

2. **Elizabeth's cat** returns at the end of the **day**.

3. **Traveling** is a great **way** to learn about other **cultures**.

4. **Afrika** shared her **secret** with her **friend**.

5. **Learning** is the **key** to finding **happiness**.

6. **Sarah's mom** asked her to tell the **joke** again.

7. **Larissa** bought her **sister** a **blouse**.

Score: _____

Name:_____   Date: _____

Grade: _____

Worksheet 1.5: Pronouns and Antecedents

Instructions: Underline each pronoun in the sentences below. Circle the antecedent.

1. Lucia borrowed her sister's brush.

2. After bathing his dog, Lucas dried her off.

3. When Kendall arrived at the party, she gave her friend a gift.

4. While walking, Tyler spotted her neighbor Pam.

5. Jack's mom asked him if he had seen the remote.

6. While learning to drive, James's father provided him with ample guidance.

7. For the holidays, Carol flew home to see her family

8. Despite his low expectations, the resort turned out to be exactly what Ben had hoped for.

9. Precious the cat played with her toy mouse all day.

10. The bird brought a worm to her babies.

Score: _____

Worksheet 1.6: Pronouns and Person

Instructions: Identify the person of the pronouns in the sentences below.

1. Our house is being cleaned, and we should leave until it is done.

2. Elizabeth packed her backpack, but she nearly forgot it on her way out the door.

3. You are going to love the party.

4. The twins may not have appeared nice, but they actually are.

5. Samantha, I got you exactly what you asked for!

6. The family was happy, and they loved each other.

7. Although the Pearson family is loud, we are all heard in our own way.

8. Jamie told her boss she could do the project, and she got it done before the deadline.

9. Colleen, here is the paperwork you asked for!

10. My dad's job is interesting, and he often tells me about his projects.

Score: _____

Name:_____   Date: _____

Grade: _____

Worksheet 1.7: Reflexive and Indefinite Pronouns

Instructions: Underline each reflective pronoun and circle each indefinite pronoun in the sentences below.

1. Clarice asked if anybody could help with her math homework.

2. Sherrie the actress watched herself on screen at the premier.

3. Nobody told Joseph that the front door would be locked.

4. Leon assured himself that everything would be okay.

5. When nobody volunteered, Thomas decided to feed the family cat himself.

6. Everyone told Jaleyah that her paper was excellent.

7. Caleb used the teacher's writing assignment to express himself.

8. After everyone else had gone to sleep, Mrs. Johnson finally took some time for herself.

9. Although her new song wasn't perfect, Arya was quite proud of herself for having written it in the first place.

10. Everyone at the party was dressed in costume, but Kacey had forgotten to make one for herself.

Score: _____

Worksheet 1.8: Relative and Interrogative Pronouns

Instructions: Underline each relative pronoun and circle each interrogative pronoun in the sentences below.

1. Treyon, who had never acted before, did very well in the school musical.

2. Whose house is painted purple and pink?

3. Who can name every U.S. state and capital?

4. Kary, whose house was pink and purple, answered the question excitedly.

5. Jakob, who was the class president, proudly displayed his knowledge to the teacher.

6. Which kind of vegetables taste best?

7. The car, which had never been taken for an oil change, broke down on the highway.

8. To whom should the gift be sent?

9. The house that hadn't been painted in 50 years finally received a fresh coat of paint.

10. Who brought these yams to our family dinner?

Score: _____

Worksheet 1.9: Verb Expressions

Instructions: In each sentence below, <u>underline</u> the verb(s) and indicate their type--physical action, mental action, linking verb, helping verb.

1. Martha dropped her plate on the floor.

2. Jay is excited to see his grandmother.

3. Cade knew not to beg.

4. The salesman persuaded the couple to purchase the new house.

5. You should go soon.

6. Mr. Frederick was my neighbor when I was 8.

7. The artist painted on her blank canvas.

8. Julie's mom considered the proposal carefully.

9. I broke a vase.

10. I would have asked the same question.

11. The CEO thought of another solution.

12. *Great Expectations* is a book by Charles Dickens.

13. Terry hugged her friend at the party.

14. Jenny wondered about her future career

15. I am who I am.

Score: _____

Name:_____ Date: _____

Grade: _____

Worksheet 1.10: Transitive and Intransitive Verbs

Instructions: Underline the verb and label it as transitive or intransitive.

1. Alessia's arm itched.

2. Simon folded his clothes.

3. Peter apologized to his sister.

4. Carrie slept.

5. Lilly painted the wall purple.

6. The ladybug jumped onto the windowsill.

7. A moth flew over the flowers.

8. Perry the penguin protected his eggs.

9. Hilly's feet ached.

10. Roger laughed jubilantly.

11. Celicia told her mom a story.

12. Victoria's questions remained.

13. Cruella wore her lavish coat.

14. The dog smiled at her owner.

15. Villains are always stopped.

Score: _____

Worksheet 1.11: Active and Passive Verbs

Instructions: Underline each verb and mark it as active or passive.

1. Silvia washed her dad's car.

2. The house was painted in two days.

3. Jessica talked to her friend on the phone.

4. The plate was broken by Janet.

5. Ricky stoked the flames in the hearth.

6. Karen hugged her mother.

7. Jordan was given a blue sweater for her birthday.

8. Many people live in the city.

9. The city is inhabited by many people.

10. Jillian's father changed the oil in her car.

11. The teacher was surprised by her student's behavior.

12. Tabitha asked her mom a question.

13. The party was abruptly ended by its host.

14. Grant asked his father for permission to go on the trip.

15. Susie the caterpillar was catapulted from the branch.

Score: _____

Worksheet 1.12: Verb Tense

Instructions: Underline each verb, and then indicate the tense of each one: past, present, future, past perfect, present perfect, future perfect.

1. Sandra went to the market.

2. David will have completed his paper by Tuesday.

3. Mark has been doing many chores around the house.

4. The car will go to the shop tomorrow.

5. Everyone is dancing at the party.

6. Maria had hoped to see her friend at the carnival.

7. Edward visited the castle.

8. Susan will have made 6 pies for the bake sale.

9. Carrie the chipmunk has been stashing many acorns.

10. The comedian is joking around.

11. William had expected more from the luncheon.

12. Tracy will have written 20 letters to her friend.

13. The Great Depression was a difficult time.

14. I am happy.

15. The CEO gave her address to the company.

Score: _____

Worksheet 1.13: Adjectives and Adverbs

Instructions: Underline each adjective and circle each adverb in the sentences below.

1. Jake peered timidly around the corner.

2. Scarlett softly pet the fluffy cat.

3. Marie drank the cool water slowly.

4. After being in the hot sun for hours, Bob was definitely ready for a cold shower!

5. Liam admired the turquoise shoes but knew he had very little money.

6. *Fahrenheit 451* is an excellent book and I would highly recommend it.

7. The twins look frighteningly similar.

8. The fancy motel was oddly inexpensive.

9. The girl laughed menacingly at the little boy.

10. Everyone politely complimented Sarah's new apartment.

11. The shy boy made a friend, much to his mother's relief.

12. Nobody understood the quirky blonde girl.

Score: _____

Name:_____   Date: _____

Grade: _____

Worksheet 1.14: What Adverbs Modify

Instructions: <u>Underline</u> each adverb and <u>indicate</u> what it is modifying (Verb, adjective, or fellow adverb) in the sentences below.

1. Martha spoke very quickly.

2. Jenny's hands were expectedly wrinkled.

3. The stewardess handed out the snacks kindly.

4. The outcome was inexplicably positive.

5. Everyone says that Candace runs quite awkwardly.

6. Noah built his house carefully.

7. Sandra's mother loved her tenderly.

8. The party was exceptionally quiet.

9. Construction workers repaved the highway very slowly.

10. Jakob's vacation felt strangely like a new life.

11. The new car was too expensive for the college student.

12. People often think too simply.

Score: _____

Name:_____   Date: _____

Grade: _____

Instructions: Circle the proper article in the sentences below.

1. A dog is (a, an, the) loyal animal.

2. Cats are (a, an, the) best animals, though.

3. The platypus is (a, an, the) egg-laying mammal.

4. Alaska is (a, an, the) biggest state in the U.S.

5. Cheryl is (a, an, the) A+ student.

6. Rhode Island is (a, an, the) very small state.

7. Alex is getting (a, an, the) updo at the salon.

8. Music is often (a, an, the) catalyst for change.

Score: _____

Name:_____   Date: _____

Grade: _____

_____

Worksheet 1.16: Prepositional Phrases

_____

Instructions: Underline the propositional phrases.

1. Kary told her mom about the party.

2. The goldfish swam around the tank.

3. Across the shore, the sun shone brightly.

4. We may never know what happened after she left.

5. The tourists climbed aboard the cruise ship.

6. The two remained friends through it all.

7. Snowball the cat played with her toy mouse.

8. Marcos decided to pour time into the new project.

9. Behind closed doors, one finds only dead ends.

10. During the play, one actress sprained her ankle.

11. Cats tend to not like people, except their owners.

12. Jake waited until the car arrived to say goodbye.

Score: _____

Name:_____   Date: _____

Grade: _____

Worksheet 1.17: Conjunctions

Instructions: <u>Underline</u> each conjunction in the sentences below, then indicate whether they are coordinating, subordinating, or correlative.

1. You must have either a permission slip or a parent's verbal approval to go on the trip.

2. Would you like tea with breakfast or would you prefer juice?

3. We will go to the park since the sun is out.

4. James and Susie wanted to play, but their parents asked them to do chores.

5. Leah wanted not only her entire family at her party, but also all of her friends.

6. Tatyanna couldn't decide between using the orange crayon and using the green one.

7. Because they delayed lunch, Noah was not able to go home to eat.

8. Since everyone was already gone, the janitor decided to listen to music while he cleaned.

9. Money doesn't bring either happiness or satisfaction.

10. I would love to go outside, yet it is raining quite hard.

Score: _____

Worksheet 1.18: Interjections and Appositives

Instructions: <u>Circle</u> the interjections and <u>underline</u> the appositives in the sentences below.

1. Mason, the quietist manager, is out for lunch.

2. Oh my, that is quite unfortunate!

3. Susie said, "Yuck!" when she opened the garbage can.

4. Hortense, the understanding landlord, extended our lease.

5. Goodness Irsula, how many hours did it take to complete that recipe?

6. The funniest girl at the table, Clarisse, made yet another killer joke.

7. Fernanda, the wisest woman in the room, gave advice to the new mother.

8. Oi, that is one big mess!

9. Oh my goodness, will this change everything?

10. The intern, a young boy from Scotland, had a passion for the trade.

11. My stars, the opportunity to be an actress is here at last!

12. Sun, the CEO of the company, is known for responding to questions with a resounding, "Ugh!"

Score: _____

Name:_____ Date: _____

Grade: _____

Instructions: Follow the prompts below. In each sentence you write, be sure to underline the words you are using to fulfill the prompt.

1: Write a sentence that includes both a common noun and a proper noun.

2: Write a sentence with a possessive noun and an appositive.

3: Write a sentence with an interrogative pronoun and a verb in the past perfect tense.

4: Write a sentence with an adverb modifying another adverb and a concrete noun.

5: Write a sentence with an indefinite pronoun and a verb in the future tense.

6: Write a sentence with a reflexive pronoun, a proper noun, and a verb in the past perfect tense.

7: Write a sentence with an intransitive verb and an adjective.

8: Write a sentence with a plural noun and an adverb modifying a verb.

9: Write a sentence with a predicate verb.

10: Write a sentence with a plural possessive noun and a prepositional phrase.

11: Write a sentence with a correlative conjunction and a mass noun.

12: Write a sentence with an interjection and an appositive.

13: Write a sentence with a singular noun and an adverb modifying an adjective.

14: Write a sentence with a possessive adjective and a verb in the present perfect tense.

15: Write a sentence with a coordinating conjunction and an interjection.

16: Write a sentence with a subordinating conjunction and a prepositional phrase.

17: Write a sentence with an article, a verb in the present tense, and second-person pronoun.

18: Write a sentence with a first person pronoun and an adverb modifying another adverb.

19: Write a sentence with an adverb modifying an adjective and a third person pronoun.

20: Write a sentence with an adverb modifying a verb, a plural noun, and a verb in the future tense.

Score: _____

Name:_____   Date: _____

Grade: _____

Unit 2: Sentences

All the exercises in this unit correspond to the Sentences chapter in *Write from the Heart: A Resource Guide to Engage Writers.*

Students can read each subsection of the chapter and complete the worksheets as follows:

Sentences Subsection	Worksheets Available
Parts of the Sentence	Worksheet 2.1: Subjects and Predicates Worksheet 2.2: Direct and Indirect Objects
Clauses and Phrases	Worksheet 2.3: Independent, Dependent, & Relative Clauses
Types of Sentences	Worksheet 2.4: Types of Sentences
Kinds of Sentences	Worksheet 2.5: Kinds of Sentences Worksheet 2.6: Sentence Summary
Summary of Unit	Unit 2 Test

Worksheet 2.1: Subjects and Predicates

Instructions: <u>Underline</u> the complete subject and <u>circle</u> the simple subject in the sentences below.

1. The young, intelligent girl dreamed of becoming a scientist.

2. A kind, helpful young man helped an elderly woman with her groceries.

3. Sofia, a software developer, created a new app.

4. Direct, honest Darnell gave excellent feedback to his employee.

5. Olgä asked her brother to play with her.

6. The patient mother made a second attempt at teaching her child.

Instructions: <u>Underline</u> the complete predicate and <u>circle</u> the simple predicate in the sentences below.

7. Hakan was very nervous about his solo.

8. Breonna has been working exceptionally hard.

9. The band was playing quite loudly.

10. The CEO spilled her burning coffee.

11. Everybody was still doing the right thing afterwards.

12. The cows had been fervently crying all night.

Score: _____

Worksheet 2.2: Direct and Indirect Objects

Instructions: <u>Underline</u> the direct objects and <u>circle</u> the indirect objects in the sentences below.

1. Cordelia handed Jamal the can opener.

2. Phil opened the can.

3. Larissa told Shay that she was upset.

4. The milkman handed the carton to the boy.

5. Noah placed the spoon into the bowl.

6. The events that occurred helped Stacey find a new sense of hope.

7. After Liu gave her mom an apology, she felt much better.

8. Kindness creates love.

9. Cars help people go fast.

10. The butler gave his employer a two-week notice.

11. Shu-Ling braided her hair.

12. Tanisha drove her car to the mechanic.

Score: _____

Worksheet 2.3: Independent, Dependent, & Relative Clauses

Instructions: Indicate whether the underlined clause is independent, dependent, or relative in the sentences below.

1. The branch fell where the children had been playing.

2. <u>Although Laila tried</u>, she could not convince her grandmother.

3. The mouse ate the cheese.

4. While an attempt was made, <u>nothing could be done</u>.

5. The cat <u>that chased away the mice</u> is named Fluffy.

6. The friend <u>who Olgä had loved</u> remained present.

7. <u>The water dripped</u> through the awning.

8. We don't have enough time to go to the carnival <u>even though you are done with your homework</u>.

9. Will you tell me when the cows come home?

10. Everyone wants what they do not have but <u>this will make them unhappy</u>.

11. Thank you for coming.

12. The children, <u>when they were questioned</u>, answered honestly.

Score: _____

Name:_____   Date: _____

Grade: _____

Worksheet 2.4: Types of Sentences

Instructions: Label each sentence below as either simple, compound, complex or compound-complex.

1. While he did apologize, his tone was not sincere, and he was looking at the ground the whole time.

2. I had to run to the store to make it before it closed.

3. When we went to the movies the other day, we really enjoyed the film.

4. The siblings hugged each other.

5. He should stay here, yet he has decided to go there.

6. Although we stayed on schedule the entire trip, we are all quite exhausted, and we didn't get the experience we were hoping for.

7. Pierre went to see his family.

8. Natalia was going to school for journalism, but now she is going for architecture.

9. Although she made a careful outline, Jazz decided to draw all over the page.

10. LaShawn is moving to New York, for he has been offered a job there.

11. Love is the answer.

12. I was initially worried about the interview, but the interviewer was really friendly and I was wearing my favorite outfit.

Score: _____

Name:_____   Date: _____

Grade: _____

Worksheet 2.5: Kinds of Sentences

Instructions: Indicate whether the sentences below are declarative, interrogative, imperative, or exclamatory.

1. What an excellent vacation!

2. What city is your new friend from?

3. I enjoy classical music.

4. Get some fresh tea from the cupboard.

5. I wish today was Friday.

6. I can't wait to get there!

7. I couldn't be more touched!

8. Do you like the gift I gave you for your birthday?

9. Don't be impolite.

10. Clean your room before we leave this afternoon.

11. Have you ever been to London?

12. I have been to London.

Score: _____

Worksheet 2.6: Sentence Summary

Instructions: Indicate the kind (declarative, interrogative, imperative, or exclamatory), voice (active or passive) and tense (present, past, future, present perfect, past perfect, or future perfect) of each sentence below.

1. The bed had been jumped on by the children.

2. Susie will have been to all 50 states by the end of the year.

3. Will anyone tell me what is going on?

4. Leave now so that you can make it back in time.

5. I can't believe you had been planning this surprise party the whole time!

6. How is anyone being deceived?

7. Make sure that the cake has been picked up by noon.

8. I wanted to go, but I couldn't.

9. The bird will be startled at the slightest noise.

10. May I go play with the other children?

Score: _____

Name:_____   Date: _____

Grade: _____

Unit 2 Test

Instructions: Follow the prompts below.

1. Write an interrogative sentence with a compound subject.

2. Write a declarative sentence with a relative clause.

3. Write a compound-complex sentence with a dependent clause.

4. Write an exclamatory sentence with an independent clause.

5. Write a declarative sentence with a compound predicate.

6. Write a complex sentence with a direct object.

7. Write a simple sentence with a relative clause and a complete predicate.

8. Write an imperative sentence with an indirect object.

9. Write an interrogative sentence with a simple predicate and an independent clause.

10. Write a compound sentence with a relative clause.

11. Write an exclamatory sentence with an indirect object.

12. Write a compound-complex sentence with an independent clause.

13. Write a complex sentence with a complete predicate.

14. Write an imperative sentence with a complete subject compound predicate.

15. Write a sentence with a compound subject and an indirect object.

16. Write a sentence with a simple subject and a direct object.

17. Write a compound sentence with a relative clause.

18. Write an exclamatory sentence with a complete predicate.

19. Write an interrogative, compound-complex sentence.

20. Write a declarative sentence with a compound predicate and an indirect object.

21. Write a sentence with a compound subject, compound predicate and indirect object.

22. Write an imperative sentence with a relative clause.

23. Write an interrogative sentence with a dependent clause.

24. Write a simple sentence with a simple subject and a simple predicate.

25. Write a complex sentence with a complete subject and predicate.

Score: _____

Unit 3: Sentence Errors

All the exercises in this unit correspond to the Sentence Errors chapter in *Write from the Heart: A Resource Guide to Engage Writers.*

Students can read each subsection of the chapter and complete the worksheets as follows:

Sentences Subsection	Worksheets Available
Fragments	Worksheet 3.1: Identifying Fragments Worksheet 3.2: Correcting Fragments
Run-ons and Comma Splices	Worksheet 3.3: Identifying Run-ons and Comma Splices Worksheet 3.4: Correcting Run-ons and Comma Splices
Rambling/Wordy Sentences	Worksheet 3.5: Rambling/Wordy Sentences
Unclear Pronoun References	Worksheet 3.6: Unclear Pronoun References
Subject-Verb Agreement	Worksheet 3.7: Subject-Verb Agreement
Misplaced and Dangling Modifiers	Worksheet 3.8: Misplaced and Dangling Modifiers
Parallelism	Worksheet 3.9: Parallelism
Summary of Unit	Unit 3 Test

Additional practice for these errors can be found in Unit 6.

Worksheet 3.1: Identifying Fragments

Instructions: Identify any fragments. If the sentence is not a fragment, mark it as correct.

1. Without a goodbye.

2. She went to the store.

3. The cat from the shelter.

4. Employees in the factory.

5. All that flour in the bowl.

6. People go to work.

7. Everyone who resides in the neighborhood.

8. The lazy dogs napped.

9. Everyone says he is kind.

10. The fox in the hen house.

Score: _____

Worksheet 3.2: Correcting Fragments

Instructions: Correct the fragments by combining the sentences.

1. Margaret's house is the next street over. On the left.

2. Because of all the parks and museums. New York is lovely.

3. That sneeze was the dog's. Not the cat's.

4. Many families enjoy the suburbs. Until their children leave home.

5. The truth is difficult to hear. Especially when it is about our character.

6. Money isn't everything. Friends too.

7. Patience is a virtue. And kindness.

8. Elizabeth was the Queen. The first one.

Score: _____

Worksheet 3.3: Identify Run-ons and Comma Splices

Instructions: Identify any run-ons and comma splices in the sentences below. If the sentence is correct, mark it "correct."

1. I built the house, she paved the driveway.

2. We bought the farm, they sold it to us.

3. We moved to the farm on Sunday our neighbors brought us an apple pie on Monday.

4. She braided my hair, my sister curled hers.

5. I opened the barn on Monday rats ran out a calf bleated.

6. When we left the city I was sad I am happier at the farm though.

7. My parents are out of town my sister and I are staying with our grandparents.

8. They shrieked, we cried.

9. I jumped, he remained still.

10. Every time I milk the cows they bleat chickens don't like the noise so they cluck angrily.

Score: _____

Worksheet 3.4: Correcting Run-ons and Comma Splices

Instructions: Correct the run-ons and comma splices.

1. I went to the theater, I was excited to see the play.

2. Shelly walked along the beach she gathered seashells.

3. It's raining outside I should probably get an umbrella.

4. I love to paint pictures, I would probably paint one every day if I could.

5. Brandon went to see his grandmother because she was sick she wasn't allowed to have visitors.

6. If you want to come to the party I need to know your preference in color I want to make sure I have the right thing for everyone.

7. My mom read my paper, she wasn't sure if I followed all the assignment requirements, though.

8. My dog jumped at the door he wanted to go out.

9. Janelle is wondering if it's okay to go to her hairdressers maybe she should just cut her hair herself.

10. Dr. Benton explained the problem to the other doctors, they listened intently.

Score: _____

Name:_____ Date: _____

Grade: _____

Worksheet 3.5: Rambling/Wordy Sentences

Instructions: Correct the rambling/wordy sentences below.

1. We went to the store, but I forgot my mask, and when I went back to the car to check for it, I realized that I left it at home.

2. The car hurdled down the road at an alarming speed, leaving onlookers in awe and asking themselves if there was anything they could have done to help stop the problem, but there probably wasn't.

3. Generation X chose to settle down and have families, but millennials have had children at much lower rates, and Generation Z is predicted to produce even fewer children in adulthood.

4. Going on road trips is a lot of fun and can be an important bonding experience, but there are many dangers of cross-country trips such as flat tires, mechanical issues, and highway hypnosis.

5. Telling the truth is difficult, but lying is even harder because you have to keep all the lies straight and if you tell one person then you have to remember what you told another person and that is really hard to do.

6. The chipmunk accused a squirrel of stealing her acorn, but it was actually a neighboring deer who was responsible for the missing acorn.

7. Some parts of the country are mountainous or near the ocean, while other parts are flat and barren, mostly in the middle of the country, but there are a few exceptions to that.

8. The earlier one begins to save money, the earlier they can retire, unless the economy is not doing well, in which case they might have to save money over a longer period of time.

Score: _____

Worksheet 3.6: Unclear Pronoun References

Instructions: Correct the unclear pronouns in the sentences below.

1. The dog and the cat sat side by side until she had to leave.

2. If you arrive after the launch time, they won't allow you on the boat..

3. Sabina and LaToya are spending the day together, but she has to stop by her house first.

4. Because the companies will be held accountable, you should keep your books properly.

5. Christine enjoyed the work, but Casey felt that she was underpaid.

6. Jacob got a B+ and Caleb got an A-, but he felt that his grade was not good enough.

7. The data showed a drop in sales and an increase in labor, but this was not reflected in the report.

8. The school announced that they will be having a picnic next week.

9. Because mental health is important, you should remember to check in with yourself frequently.

10. Ronald was loud and did not apologize, which was frustrating.

Score: _____

Name:_____ Date: _____

Grade: _____

Worksheet 3.7: Subject-Verb Agreement

Instructions: Circle the correct subject/verb to complete the sentences below.

1. Sasha (is / are) a fluffy gray dog.

2. Many people at the party (think / thinks) the music is enjoyable.

3. The Hankins (was / were) a happy family.

4. Sugar (rot / rots) your teeth in excess.

5. Raindrops (is / are) cool and refreshing.

6. Rhea and Midori (like / likes) watching TV together.

7. Everyone at the play (delight / delights) in the performance.

8. The tablet or the paper (is / are) in the drawer.

9. My mom, as well as all us children, (has / have) curly hair.

10. The boy with all the action figures (bring / brings) his toys to share.

Score: _____

Worksheet 3.8: Misplaced and Dangling Modifiers

Instructions: Correct the misplaced/dangling modifiers in the sentences below.

1. Tom saw a large Sequoia driving through the forest.

2. Rollerskating down the driveway, the wheel came off the skate.

3. The rope felt secure while climbing up the mountain.

4. Heather nearly sang every minute of the day.

5. I ate a large sandwich reading a book.

6. Writing down the checklist, the pen ran out of ink.

7. Bill saw three dogs on his front porch.

8. Only William gave me $10 to paint the whole porch.

9. Waiting in anticipation, the door opened and it was my sister.

10. Jamie saw a butterfly laying in her hammock in the woods.

Score: _____

Worksheet 3.9: Parallelism

Instructions: Correct the parallelism errors in the sentences below.

1. At the game, we danced, ate pickles, and were cheering for the team.

2. I like to read more than going to the movies.

3. Being a teacher is both difficult and it is rewarding.

4. Jillian danced, was talking, and helped clean up at the party.

5. This is either a terrible notion or it could be a really good plan.

6. Mark enjoys skiing more than the shops.

7. Reneé is making either pancakes or she is making waffles.

8. Janelle sang, was cheering on other singers, and encouraged her partner at the competition.

Score: _____

Name:_____   Date: _____

Grade: _____
_____

Unit 3 Test
_____

Instructions: Using the list, identify the errors in the paragraph below.

1 Rambling/Wordy

1 Run-On

3 Comma Splices

2 Fragments

1 Unclear Pronoun Reference

2 Subject/Verb Agreement Errors

1 Misplaced Modifier

It are not uncommon for two people to gaze upon the same picture but see it in completely

unique ways, and this is the case with Hamlet and Willy because it cannot be argued that either of

them made good choices. They fail to see the hurt they are causing doing whatever they want.

Both of their goals contribute to much personal suffering and hurt those around them too. The

difference between these two men. Hamlet thinks through his plans and considers their impact

every time, Willy make choices without considering their effect on others. Both men who made

mistakes. They both face tough circumstances, but Hamlet chooses to channel grief into action,

Willy refuses to accept the consequences of his actions.

Name:_____   Date: _____

Grade: _____

Instructions: Identify the errors in the paragraph below. They include: Rambling/Wordy Sentences, Run-On and Comma Splices, Fragments, Unclear Pronoun References, Subject/Verb Agreement Errors, and Misplaced Modifiers. There are 14 total errors

In walking through their lives and mental processes, it becomes quite clear that both men are control by the events that the plays are based around. For Hamlet it are the deception of his father at the hands of his uncle and his mother's swift friendship to him. Because he cannot accept the new state of his life. Hamlet starts down a path of vengeance and anger from which he knows that he cannot return, but a rational man would not take such foolish and dangerous actions that could only end in tragedy for himself and those around him. Hamlet was blinded by his grief, Willy are a man who regrets his past actions and feels as if he has fallen short of his goals. Willy cannot accept his mistakes and appreciate the good things that his choices have brought, which is evidenced by his delusional state of mind and deflective speech, for instance, Willy's older son Biff catch him in the midst of a lie. Instead of fessing up to his lie, Willy simply become angry at Biff for running away in tears. Biff goes downhill after this, but Willy refuses to recognize his part in it. As Biff returns home a decade later, Willy's delusions worsen severely. He allows his fantasy of success to go too far, is unstable, and was not being realistic. Living in denial, his life fell apart. A more stable person would have simply made incremental lifestyle changes to accommodate their goal, Willy is all about instant gratification and it holds him back. Hamlet and Willy have similar fates, but he gets to them through different means.

Score: _____

Unit 4: Comma Punctuation

All the exercises in this unit correspond to the Comma Punctuation chapter in *Write from the Heart: A Resource Guide to Engage Writers.*

Students can read each subsection of the chapter and complete the worksheets as follows:

Sentences Subsection	Worksheets Available
Lists	Worksheet 4.1: Lists
Compound Sentences	Worksheet 4.2: Coordinating Conjunctions
Dependent Clauses	Worksheet 4.3: Dependent Clauses
Interjections and Appositives	Worksheet 4.4: Interjections and Appositives
Addresses and Dates	Worksheet 4.5: Addresses and Dates
Summary of Unit	Unit 4 Test

Additional practice for these skills can be found in Unit 6.

Worksheet 4.1: Lists

Instructions: Correct the comma/list errors in the sentences below.

1. Lauren wrote papers about her parents the first man to walk on the moon and a famous actress.

2. Before he went to school, he got dressed fixed his hair and ate breakfast.

3. I went walking with my best friend my dog and my little sister.

4. On my birthday, I want to go for a hike eat lots of cake and have a sleepover with my friends.

5. My dad asked me to take care of my brothers the dog and the cat while he is away.

6. I eat breakfast lunch and dinner every day.

7. Jenny invited her three cousins Susan and Joe to the party.

8. Rachel likes baking collecting coins and riding horses.

Score: _____

Worksheet 4.2: Coordinating Conjunctions

Instructions: Add appropriate commas and coordinating conjunctions (FANBOYS) to connect the sentences below.

1. I went to the store. My sister asked me to pick up avocados.

2. She left the country. She never forgot where she came from.

3. True apologies are difficult. They require genuine remorse.

4. We could go rollerskating. We could go ice skating.

5. My parents took me to a theme park. Then they bought me dinner.

6. My older brother is 18. My younger brother is 12.

7. We can't go to the beach. We can't go to the mountains.

8. The resort is quite expensive. I still desire to go.

Score: _____

Worksheet 4.3: Dependent Clauses

Instructions: Place proper commas in the sentences below if they are needed.

1. Although she never expected it Lana became a movie star.

2. Before he left for work Steve helped his kids with their homework.

3. Since Sarah said yes Beth put her to work right away.

4. I watered all the plants since it hasn't rained in three days.

5. Although James had not expected it the job opportunity prompted him to move to San Francisco.

6. Unlike her old friends Jane fell in love with her cool new friends.

7. Riddhi wanted to surprise her husband with a trip although she knew it would be tricky.

8. Since the party was busy Alex chose to bring everyone into the backyard.

9. Although the airplane had not even taken off several passengers were becoming nervous.

10. While it had not been planned the trip to the waterpark was quite fun.

Score: _____

Worksheet 4.4: Transition Phrases

Instructions: Place proper commas in the sentences below if they are needed.

1. Tom however didn't find the music to his liking.

2. In summary it is important that we all wash our hands.

3. She was late again of course.

4. In the first place the sloppiness of my roommate is rather disrespectful.

5. Next we will marinate the meat for the barbeque tomorrow.

6. The most important thing then is to make sure your kids know you love them.

7. My father meanwhile always falls asleep three-quarters of the way through the movie.

8. Otherwise it will be impossible to find our keys again.

9. When Ruby gave me her necklace to wear, I knew she trusted me finally.

10. Besides there are lots of times when we have to work hard.

Score: _____

Worksheet 4.5: Interjections and Appositives

Instructions: Add commas to correct the sentences below.

1. Wow the garbage smells really bad.

2. Julia our babysitter makes great peanut butter cookies.

3. Eugene I would like you to take the dog for a walk.

4. I want to play with the green car not the purple one when Timmy comes over this evening.

5. I burned my finger yesterday, and ouch it hurts!

6. I just made a lasagna for Maria our neighbor.

7. Oh no it's starting to rain!

8. You are supposed to use basil not oregano in that recipe

9. My two brothers Thomas and Dean helped us move into our new house

10. Gee it's a long walk to get to the waterfall.

Score: _____

Name:_____   Date: _____

Grade: _____

Worksheet 4.6: Addresses and Dates

Instructions: Add or remove commas to correct the sentences below.

1. Maya was born on January 12 1999.

2. On our road trip, we stopped at 7477 Hubbard Avenue Middleton Wisconsin 53562.

3. Nathan is coming to visit us in June, 2021.

4. The wedding will take place on September 7 2020 at the event center.

5. Trent's family lived at 855 Visionary Trail Golden Colorado 80401 before they moved away.

6. The date of December 7 1941 is a "day that will live in infamy."

7. I entered 114 North Main Street Roswell New Mexico 88203 into my navigation system.

8. We will celebrate Mildred's birthday in April, 2021.

Score: _____

Unit 4 Test

Part 1

Instructions: Place commas in the proper places in the sentences below. There are 14 commas needed.

The day I visited my Aunt Sally

I walked to my Aunt Sally's house on May 21 1998 6 weeks before my 12th birthday. Before I arrived

she made sure to have all of my favorite snacks and games ready. Her home was a lovely old house

with ivy growing on the front wall sitting proudly at 2323 Main Street Brooklyn New York 10001.

Gee it was a lovely house! As soon as I walked in the aroma of fresh baked cookies met my nostrils

sweetly and I heard my aunt humming quietly in the kitchen. When I entered the kitchen she

gave me a big hug and sat me down at the table for cookies and games. I won at Monopoly but she

beat me soundly at spades. We also played chess Jenga and checkers. It was an amazing day. This

particular aunt who lived with my family when I was a baby was my favorite aunt growing up.

Part 2

Instructions: Write sentences with commas as instructed.

1. Write a sentence that includes a list of three items.

2. Write a compound sentence that uses a coordinating conjunction.

3. Write a sentence that begins with a dependent clause.

4. Write a sentence with an interjection.

5. Write a sentence that includes an appositive.

6. Write a sentence that includes a transition word.

7. Write a sentence with an address in it, including the street name, city, state, and zip code.

8. Write a sentence that has a date in it, including a month, day, and year.

Score: _____

Unit 5: Other Punctuation

All the exercises in this unit correspond to the Other Punctuation chapter in *Write from the Heart: A Resource Guide to Engage Writers.*

Students can read each subsection of the chapter and complete the worksheets as follows:

Sentences Subsection	Worksheets Available
Capitalization	Worksheet 5.1: Capitalization
Titles	Worksheet 5.2: Titles
Hypens, Dashes, Parentheses, Brackets, Ellipses, Colons	Worksheet 5.3: Punctuating with Variety
Semicolons	Worksheet 5.4: Semicolons
Apostrophes	Worksheet 5.5: Apostrophes
Summary of Unit	Worksheet 5.6: Punctuation and Sentence Summary Unit 5 Test

Worksheet 5.1: Capitalization

Instructions: Correct the capitalization errors in the sentences below. Some errors need to be capitalized, and others need to have the capital removed.

1. I have a dentist's appointment on wednesday afternoon.

2. My grandparents' names are lucas and patricia.

3. they went to the grocery store yesterday.

4. My history class is taking a field trip to philadelphia in august.

5. In the show that i watch, the country is led by president robertson.

6. I decided to drive East on my road trip.

7. I bought the perfect gift for mom this christmas.

8. Julie and i are having lunch sometime this Summer.

9. My birthday is in july.

10. The bill was just signed by governor butterfield.

11. This Winter, my Dad and i are traveling to maine.

12. My friend bobby lives South of me.

Score: _____

Worksheet 5.2: Titles

Instructions: Re-write each underlined title below using appropriate grammar rules. The context of the sentence will tell you what type of title it is.

1. In the play the death of a salesman, Willie Lowman has to come to terms with mistakes he made in his life.

2. One of my favorite books is anne of green gables because the main character is not perfect and is so relatable.

3. In the 1980s, many celebrities helped raise money by participating in the recording of the song we are the world.

4. Edgar Allen Poe's short story the tell-tale heart is an example of a story told by an unreliable narrator.

5. As a child, I would watch and rewatch the princess bride because it was such a good movie.

6. The poem i, too, sing america is by Langston Hughes.

7. The song yellow is my favorite track on Coldplay's album parachutes.

8. Have you seen the remake of the Disney movie the lion king?

Score: _____

Worksheet 5.3: Punctuating with Variety

Instructions: Re-write each sentence below using a dash, parentheses, ellipses, or a colon.

1. Lana, who had been a journalist, decided to become an author.

2. The wait was certainly longer than we anticipated—impatience abounded.

3. George (born in 1991) is considered a millennial.

4. Scarcity leadership is not leadership at all.

5. Only buy the things from the list.

6. Leslie decided to move to California last November.

7. Lïsle chose to stay in Sweden during the winter.

8. LaQuisha loves her work as a doctor.

9. Even in the face of difficult circumstances, there is only the truth.

10. I went to the salon and got a fresh perm.

Score: _____

Worksheet 5.4: Semicolons

Instructions: Combine the content of each set of sentences using semicolons.

1. I am so happy that I finally won a prize. I have been training for months.

2. I have cousins in Atlanta, Georgia. I have cousins in Bangor, Maine. I have cousins in Detroit, Michigan.

3. I lived in Switzerland for 20 years. It was an incredible experience.

4. My mom makes baklava when I come home. She makes it better than anyone else.

5. The dog barked at the cat. They don't get along.

6. Susie the caterpillar climbed up the fence. She did it every Sunday,

7. Läslow the marmot scampered away. The hikers scared her.

8. Mice often burrow in small spaces. They hide well.

Score: _____

Worksheet 5.5: Apostrophes

Instructions: Place apostrophes in the appropriate spots in the sentences below.

1. The familys cat hissed.

2. Her moms new blouse was ripped.

3. The Gildans home was blown away in the tornado.

4. Janes house is blue.

5. The car ran over roberts foot.

Instructions: Write the proper contraction in place of the emboldened words.

6. The twins **have not** been to the theme park.

7. Jake **would not** tell a lie.

8. Susan **will not** be at the party.

9. **You are** my best friend.

10. **It is** Sunday.

Score: _____

Worksheet 5.6: Punctuation and Sentence Summary

Instructions: Combine the sentences in each set together in TWO different ways. You can have more than one sentence, but several should be combined. Feel free to change their structure (endings of nouns or verbs, add in a coordinating conjunction or dependent word, adding transitions, etc). Use proper punctuation. You will have two collections of sentences for each set.

Set A

- Jessie washed his mom's car.

- There was neither soap nor rags in the garage.

- The neighbor's sprinklers were spraying onto the driveway.

- The car was very dirty.

- Jessie's mom was very thankful.

Set B

- Lolly wanted to become a lawyer.

- She worked hard throughout college.

- Lolly was accepted to a prestigious law school.

- Once she graduated, she fought for justice.

- Lolly liked her job.

Set C

- Jasmine asked for a scarf for her birthday.

- Her parents pretended to forget what she wanted.

- Jasmine felt disappointed.

- On her birthday, Jasmine's parents gave her the scarf.

- Jasmine was overjoyed.

Set D

- Bob built a new building.

- Bob's building was 500 feet tall.

- Bob made his new building into an office.

- The office became successful.

- Bob was proud of his building.

Score: _____

Grade: _____

Unit 5 Test

Instructions: Follow the prompts below.

- Write a sentence that contains brackets.

- Write a sentence that contains a title.

- Write a sentence that contains an apostrophe.

- Write a sentence that contains an ellipsis.

- Write a sentence that contains a semicolon.

- Write a sentence that contains a colon.

- Write a sentence that contains parentheses.

- Write a sentence that contains an em dash.

- Write a sentence that contains an en dash.

- Write a sentence that contains a hyphen.

- Write a sentence that contains a capitalized word.

- Write a sentence that contains an apostrophe and brackets.

Name:_____   Date: _____

Grade: _____

- Write a sentence that contains a semicolon and an ellipsis.

- Write a sentence that contains a hyphen and a title.

- Write a sentence that contains an en dash and a capitalized word.

- Write a sentence that contains a colon and title.

- Write a sentence that contains an em dash and brackets.

- Write a sentence that contains a hyphen.

- Write a sentence that contains parentheses and a title.

- Write a sentence that contains an apostrophe and a capitalized word.

- Write a sentence that contains a semicolon.

- Write a sentence that contains an em dash.

- Write a sentence that contains an en dash.

- Write a sentence that contains parentheses and a colon.

- Write a sentence that contains an ellipsis.

Score: _____

Unit 6: Additional Improvement Practice

This unit combines many of the skills learned in the other units for additional student practice of the concepts in *Write from the Heart: A Resource Guide to Engage Writers.*

Students can read each subsection of the chapter and complete the worksheets as follows:

Skills Practiced	Worksheets Available
Fragments	Worksheet 6.1: Fragments Worksheet 6.9: Essay Editing 1 Worksheet 6.10: Essay Editing 2
Comma Splices & Run-ons	Worksheet 6.2: Run-ons and Comma Splices Worksheet 6.9: Essay Editing 1 Worksheet 6.10: Essay Editing 2
Rambling and Wordy Sentences	Worksheet 6.3: Rambling and Wordy Sentences Worksheet 6.9: Essay Editing 1 Worksheet 6.10: Essay Editing 2
Unclear Pronouns	Worksheet 6.4: Unclear Pronouns Worksheet 6.9: Essay Editing 1
Subject-Verb Agreement	Worksheet 6.5: Subject-Verb Agreement Worksheet 6.9: Essay Editing 1
Misplaced and Dangling Modifiers	Worksheet 6.6: Misplaced and Dangling Modifiers Worksheet 6.9: Essay Editing 1 Worksheet 6.10: Essay Editing 2
Parallelism	Worksheet 6.7: Parallelism Worksheet 6.9: Essay Editing 1
Commas	Worksheet 6.8: Commas Worksheet 6.9: Essay Editing 1 Worksheet 6.10: Essay Editing 2
Capitalization, Titles, Apostrophes	Worksheet 6.10: Essay Editing 2

Worksheet 6.1: Fragments

Instructions: Correct the fragments in this paragraph.

Herbology is the study of plants. Herbology as a hobby. Being an herbalist requires a deep love for

plants. Most understand various uses and ways. To care for plants. While many are searching for

healthier and more natural ways of living. Herbology is becoming more and more prominent.

Score: _____

Worksheet 6.2: Run-Ons and Comma Splices

Instructions: Correct the run-ons and comma splices in this paragraph.

The Mainstreet Dog Park is a very nice place, a lot of people in town enjoy visiting it with their dogs. I enjoy the shaded seating and multiple watering spots. My dog, Lucky, a feisty chocolate lab, became friends with another dog, Fido, they played for hours on our first visit and even longer the second visit. Frank, Fido's owner, is a nice guy, he lives a few blocks away, his apartment is right around the corner from my favorite ice cream place. Going to the dog park is a regular event for Lucky and me, we both love a lot of things it offers and intend to keep going for the rest of the summer.

Score: _____

Worksheet 6.3: Rambling and Wordy Sentences

Instructions: Correct the rambling and wordy sentences in this paragraph.

Teaching is a challenging profession, and it requires much of those who work in it and oftentimes requires big trade-offs, both personally, financially and professionally. In other careers, you may get long coffee breaks, flexible lunch breaks, and chances to socialize throughout the day.

Teaching, especially in lower elementary, rarely gives you the time to chat with coworkers. It is no secret that teaching is also an underpaid profession, as teachers also frequently have to use their own funds to purchase needed supplies such as crayons, pencils, kleenex, markers, and other craft supplies. Finally, teaching is a taxing profession and the amount of work and long hours limit opportunities to pursue further schooling and professional development. These challenges are large and difficult but do not diminish the many benefits and joys that come with teaching as a profession.

Score: _____

Worksheet 6.4: Unclear Pronouns

Instructions: Correct the unclear pronouns in this paragraph.

To Kill a Mockingbird by Harper Lee is considered by some to be an important and essential book.

Across the country, many students read the book in their classrooms and engage in conversations

around the subject matter. It leads to important discussions on race, justice, and involvement in

the community. Teachers often craft various lessons around the book, which helps you delve

deeper into the content. They frequently speak of the lasting impact it has in the classrooms. For

many, *To Kill a Mockingbird* is an important text to complete and learn from. This is what sets this

text apart from many other books read throughout schools in this country.

Score: _____

Worksheet 6.5: Subject-Verb Agreement

Instructions: Correct the verbs that don't agree with their subject in this paragraph.

My mother, Taraji, celebrate Kwanza every December. It is an important holiday for her and our family. Kwanza is focused on seven principles, and they is: *Umoja, Kujichagulia, Ujima, Ujamaa, Nia, Kuumba, Imani*. Each of these principles are celebrated one a day, for all seven days of the holiday's season. These principles translates to mean: unity, self-determination, collective work, cooperative economics, purpose, creativity, and faith. Maulana Karenga, the creator of the Holiday, wanted a holiday for African Americans that was separate from Christmas and provided a space solely for the African-American community to celebrate and come together. My mother believe in that vision and continue the tradition in our family. She hope I do the same with my future family.

Score: _____

Name:_____ Date: _____

Grade: _____

Worksheet 6.6: Misplaced and Dangling Modifiers

Instructions: Correct the misplaced and dangling modifiers in this paragraph.

There are many types of cats in this world. My favorite breed is the Russian Blue. Russian Blues are

known for silky blue-ish fur and yellow eyes. I first saw a Russian Blue walking past a local

bookstore. The cat caught my attention actually because of its color and size. With bulky fur, I just

want to pet one. Another aspect of this breed is they are hypoallergenic, which cause flare-ups for

folks rarely allergic to cats. Both beautiful and friendly, I think this makes them a great option for

a pet.

Score: _____

Worksheet 6.7: Parallelism

Instructions: Correct the parallelism errors in this paragraph.

I love going to the movies. The local movie theater has everything you could want: exciting movies, food that fills you up, refreshing air conditioning, and relaxing seats. During the summer it is the most popular spot to be. Oftentimes you can see many friends going together. They might be looking for a fun activity that gets them out of the heat, or they want to see a new movie. Either way, it is the place to be. The local theater offers plenty of fun and amenities to the community.

Score: _____

Worksheet 6.8: Commas

Instructions: Correct the comma errors in these paragraphs. The number of commas needed are marked at the end of the paragraphs.

John Locke a philosopher in the 1600's lived in England during a troubled time. Many people who disagreed with the monarchy's free reign were arrested and sometimes killed. Because of his ideas that rulers of a country have limited power Locke was forced to flee England to save his life. Years later Locke was finally free to write down his ideas when King William and Queen Mary initiated a constitutional monarchy. A constitutional monarchy is a monarchy where the king has to obey rules laid down by Parliament an elected legislature. This was different from the former monarchy where the monarch had no accountability. (6)

John Locke's ideas influenced other countries like America and France. The American Revolution began in the 1770's sparked by the king of England King George III and his tyranny towards America. After the Revolutionary War Locke's ideas were used as the foundation of the American Constitution. After America broke away from England the French who had helped America fight during the revolution saw the application and benefits of Locke's ideas in the colonies. After returning from the war in the colonies the French became more and more discontent with the absolute monarch that ruled their country. The French revolted and successfully got rid of their king. (9)

Score: _____

Worksheet 6.9: Essay Editing 1

Instructions: Label the following errors in these paragraphs: fragments, run-ons, comma splices, subject-verb agreement, misplaced or dangling modifiers, rambling or wordy sentences, and parallelism errors. Circle any word that needs a comma after it. Optional: Re-write the essay with the errors corrected. Total of 25 errors--the number of errors in each paragraph is marked at the end of the paragraph..

Animal Crossing: New Horizons and Its Popularity

Video games has become increasingly more and more popular as time goes on. There are countless types of games, from platforming games to role-playing games. Many folks who play them have their own specific tastes. Occasionally a video game will come around at the right time and pick-up a lot of fans, even folks that previously did not play that sort of game. That is what occurred on the launch date of *Animal Crossing: New Horizons*. A video game that became a huge piece of pop culture and a worldwide phenomenon. (5)

The Animal Crossing series has a lengthy history. The first version was released in Japan. Right before the launch of the Nintendo Gamecube. After that first version was released it steadily picked up fans and released new versions on a regular basis. The concept of the game is simple you are placed in a small village with animal neighbors and can engage in various activities like fishing and bug-catching. For many this game is considered peaceful and relaxing and offers a break from other louder and more action-packed video games. (4)

With every new release of Animal Crossing, the developers offer new features and gameplay for players to engage with because it's fun and everyone seems to like it so they keep putting them out. Although it had a dedicated group of fans, it never became as mainstream as other Nintendo titles like the Pokemon series or Mario games. It would change in 2020. In late 2019 Nintendo announced an upcoming release of the newest Animal Crossing game, *New Horizons*. It was met with celebration by its fanbase and was eagerly awaited. The newest version was released on March 20 2020 which coincided with a sudden increase in stay-at-home orders and social distancing rules related to the international COVID-19 outbreak. (7)

This caused a sharp uptick in sales and popularity. Many folks found the game's relaxed gameplay a perfect respite from increasingly what was becoming a more difficult and scarier world. Social media was flooded with images of folks holding online graduation ceremonies, weddings, recreating popular game shows, and talk shows. The excitement was only further increased as more of the game's features were discovered such as terra-forming a landscaping feature that allows for full customization. The game's popularity began to draw folks that traditionally played other genres of video games or was not video game players prior to the release. (5)

Animal Crossing: New Horizons is a great example of a video game gaining mass popularity. Not only did the game have a solid fanbase prior to its launch but it also picked up new fans and new gamers due world events. The game offered a perfect space to play, create, and relax while offering opportunities to interact digitally with friends while maintaining social distancing. For these reasons *Animal Crossing: New Horizons* will most likely maintain its status in pop culture and be a video game that many will remember. (4)

Score: _____

Worksheet 6.10: Essay Editing 2

Instructions: Label sentence and punctuation errors in this essay. Label the sentence errors. Circle any word that needs a comma after it. Underline punctuation errors. Optional: Re-write the essay with the errors corrected.

Total of 30 errors throughout the essay in these categories:
Fragments, run-ons, comma splices (xx) 5
Subject-verb agreement (xx) 2
Misplaced or dangling modifiers (xx) 2
Rambling or wordy sentences (xx) 2
Comma errors (xx) 12
Punctuation errors—Capitalization, titles, apostrophes (xx) 7

Jane Austen Book Recommendation

Catherine Morland, the main character in Jane Austen's novel Northanger Abbey, is forced to endure numerous harsh trials throughout her story. Although this is hard for her it results in a maturity beyond her years in one scenario she must share quarters with a suspected murderer. Or worse. In another, the person she only loves catches her in a foolish act. And at one point, she must use all her mental and physical strength to do something that brings displeasure to her brother and dearest friends. It seems that everything she does anything she thinks and all the people she interacts with brings harm upon her or a loved one. Is Austen kind enough to let her main character live a happy ending? The answer to this question is played out wonderfully in Northanger Abbey, intermingled with inspiring gothic themes.

Jane Austen uses adventure and mystery as a prominent gothic element in her novel by creating a chilling suspense in the reader and it's all very unsettling and creepy. Such creepy adventures includes a visit to a large and ominous abbey which is the main source of the intrigue. General Tilney is the person who runs it, Catherine strays from the grounds of common sense and is tempted to suspect the Generals motives. But even more mysterious are the large locked chests Catherine discovers in her room. The foreboding hallway which leads to the door of the deceased Mrs. Tilneys bedroom. Imagining dark things, the ideas Catherine comes up earn her dire consequences.

Another striking theme in the book Northanger Abbey is the study of the inner self. Catherine is posed with several opportunities to judge. Between true love and deceptive infatuation. Even her closest friend Isabella someone she would never have dreamed to be an outright liar ends up lying to her face more than once. And Catherine herself is forced to decide whether to go on an outing with friends or wait for her stuffy hosts. The author ingeniously deals with the difficult situations which tear at Catherines soul. If she makes a bad decision her guilt will ruin the days that pass until she sets it straight.

Perhaps the most important element in Austen's novel is her own commentary on gothic novels of her time. Nowadays it seems to be unacceptable for the author to openly comment on other people's tastes while the story is still in the middle of the action, but that is what Austen does and she gives her view on gothic novels and culture of her time. In several places she exaggerate her own story in order to poke fun at the stupidity of other novels. While slightly amusing, her spicy comments are helpful when you are looking for a better understanding of gothic literature of the 18th century. In fact it seems that Jane Austens whole purpose when writing her story was to provide the world with an extensive knowledge of her opinions.

I recommend Northanger Abbey as an excellent gothic novel to read. It is full of stimulating adventures emotional introspection of the human heart and wonderful opportunities to get a first-hand biased view on gothic literature.

Score: _____

Grammar Answer Keys

Unit 1: Parts of Speech

Worksheet 1.1: Common Nouns vs. Proper Nouns
(Common nouns are bolded; proper nouns are underlined)
1. I want to travel to many different **countries**, but especially <u>France</u>.
2. <u>Chloe</u> attended <u>Stanford University</u> for her college **degree**.
3. <u>Sam</u>'s favorite **season** is **summer**, but she was born in <u>January</u>.
4. <u>Terry</u>'s favorite **place** to go for a special **treat** is <u>McDonald's</u>.
5. My **brother**'s favorite **holiday** is <u>Easter</u>, but my favorite **holiday** is the <u>Fourth of July</u>.
6. Sometimes, **communication** in my **family** is confusing, because my **mom**'s name is <u>Joan</u>, and my **aunt**'s name is <u>Jean</u>.
7. One of my favorite **things** to do in my spare **time** is to play <u>Mario Kart</u>.
8. Someday, our **family** would like to visit <u>New York City</u> to see the <u>Empire State Building</u> and the <u>Statue of Liberty</u>.
9. What <u>Grandma</u> said at **dinner** made the whole **family** very emotional.
10. We are going to see the **fireworks** that <u>John</u> is setting off.

Worksheet 1.2: Concrete Nouns vs. Abstract Nouns
In the following sentences, label each noun as either concrete or abstract.
(abstract nouns are bolded; concrete nouns are underlined)
1. <u>Abraham Lincoln</u> is famously remembered as never being able to tell a **lie**.
2. The <u>eagle</u> in the <u>United States</u> represents **freedom**.
3. <u>Owls</u> are often portrayed in <u>stories</u>, <u>movies</u>, and <u>cartoons</u> as having **intelligence**.
4. <u>Gifts</u> are wonderful, but **kindness** means more to me.
5. My little <u>brother</u> was in **pain**, but the <u>BandAid</u> made him feel better.
6. How the <u>cat</u> learned to operate the <u>icemaker</u> is still a **mystery** to me.
7. We love where we vacation each <u>summer</u> because it is so **beautiful**.
8. I don't know why the <u>song</u> brings me such **joy**, but I can't stop listening to it.
9. Whoever ate the last piece of <u>cake</u> probably has chocolate <u>lips</u> that will reveal the **truth**.
10. My <u>parents</u> can be **strict**, but I know it is out of **love**.

Worksheet 1.3: Singular vs. Plural vs. Mass Nouns
1. **Money** isn't everything. (Mass)
2. The **teacher** instructed the **students**. (Sing., Plu.)
3. They asked the **family** about all their **trips**. (Sing., Plu.)
4. The **cars** all rolled to a stop. (Plu.)
5. The **child** hugged her **mother**. (Sing., Sing.)
6. **Happiness** is fleeting, but never gone forever. (Mass)
7. **Women** make up slightly more than half of the U.S. **population**. (Plu., Sing.)
8. **Time** heals most **wounds**. (Mass, Plu.)

Worksheet 1.4: Uses of Nouns
1. The **mom** called her **son** to the kitchen. (subject, object)
2. **Elizabeth**'s **cat** returns at the end of the **day**. (poss., subject, object)
1. **Traveling** is a great **way** to learn about other **cultures**. (subject, pred., object)
2. **Afrika** shared her **secret** with her **friend**. (subject, object, object)

3. **Learning** is the **key** to finding **happiness**. (subject, pred., object)
4. **Sarah's mom** asked her to tell the **joke** again. (poss., subject, object)
5. **Larissa** bought her **sister** a **blouse**. (subject, object, object)

Worksheet 1.5 Pronouns and Antecedents

Pronouns are underlined and antecedents are bolded.

1. **Lucia** borrowed <u>her</u> sister's brush.
2. After bathing <u>his</u> **dog, Lucas** dried <u>her</u> off. (dog=her; Lucas=him)
3. When **Kendall** arrived at the party, <u>she</u> gave <u>her</u> friend a gift.
4. While walking, **Tyler** spotted <u>his</u> neighbor Pam.
5. **Jack**'s mom asked <u>him</u> if <u>he</u> had seen the remote.
6. While learning to drive, **James**'s father provided <u>him</u> with ample guidance.
7. For the holidays, **Carol** flew home to see <u>her</u> family
8. Despite <u>his</u> low expectations, the resort turned out to be exactly what **Ben** had hoped for.
9. **Precious the cat** played with <u>her</u> toy mouse all day.
10. The **bird** brought a worm to <u>her</u> babies.

Worksheet 1.6: Pronouns and Person
1. Our house is being cleaned, and we should leave until it is done. (1st)
2. Elizabeth packed her backpack, but she nearly forgot it on her way out the door. (3rd)
3. You are going to love the party. (2nd)
4. The twins may not have appeared nice, but they actually are. (3rd)
5. Samantha, I got you exactly what you asked for! (2nd)
6. The family was happy, and they loved each other. (3rd)
7. Although the Pearson family is loud, we are all heard in our own way. (1st)

8. Jamie told her boss she could do the project, and she got it done before the deadline. (3rd)
9. Colleen, here is the paperwork you asked for! (2nd)
10. My dad's job is interesting, and he often tells me about his projects. (3rd, 1st)

Worksheet 1.7 Reflexive and Indefinite

Reflexive pronouns are underlined, and indefinite pronouns are bolded.

1. Clarice asked if **anybody** could help with her math homework.
2. Sherrie the actress watched <u>herself</u> on screen at the premier.
3. **Nobody** told Joseph that the front door would be locked.
4. Leon assured <u>himself</u> that everything would be okay.
5. When **nobody** volunteered, Thomas decided to feed the family cat <u>himself</u>.
6. **Everyone** told Jaleyah that her paper was excellent.
7. Caleb used the teacher's writing assignment to express <u>himself</u>.
8. After **everyone** else had gone to sleep, Mrs. Johnson finally took some time for <u>herself</u>.
9. Although her new song wasn't perfect, Arya was quite proud of <u>herself</u> for having written it in the first place.
10. **Everyone** at the party was dressed in costume, but Kacey had forgotten to make one for <u>herself</u>.

Worksheet 1.8: Relative and Interrogative

Relative pronouns are underlined, and interrogative pronouns are bolded.

1. Treyon, <u>who</u> had never acted before, did very well in the school musical.
2. **Whose** house is painted purple and pink?
3. **Who** can name every U.S. state and

capital?

4. Kary, <u>whose</u> house was pink and purple, answered the question excitedly.
5. Jakob, <u>who</u> was the class president, proudly displayed his knowledge to the teacher.
6. **Which** kind of vegetables taste best?
7. The car, <u>which</u> had never been taken for an oil change, broke down on the highway.
8. To **whom** should the gift be sent?
9. The <u>house</u> that hadn't been painted in 50 years finally received a fresh coat of paint.
10. **Who** brought these yams to our family dinner?

Worksheet 1.9: Verb Expressions

1. Martha **<u>dropped</u>** her plate on the floor. (Physical Action)
2. Jay **<u>is excited</u>** to see his grandmother. (Linking Verb, Mental Action)
3. Cade **<u>knew</u>** not to **<u>beg</u>**. (Mental Action, Physical Action)
4. The salesman **<u>persuaded</u>** the couple to **<u>purchase</u>** the new house. (Mental Action, Physical Action)
5. You **<u>should go</u>** soon. (Helping Verb, Physical Action)
6. Mr. Frederick **<u>was</u>** my neighbor when I **<u>was</u>** 8. (Linking Verb, Linking Verb)
7. The artist **<u>painted</u>** on her blank canvas. (Physical Action)
8. Julie's mom **<u>considered</u>** the proposal carefully. (Mental Action)
9. I **<u>broke</u>** a vase. (Physical Action)
10. I **<u>would have asked</u>** the same question. (Helping Verb(s), Physical Action)
11. The CEO **<u>thought</u>** of another solution. (Mental Action)
12. *Great Expectations* **<u>is</u>** a book by Charles Dickens. (Linking Verb)
13. Terry **<u>hugged</u>** her friend at the party. (Physical Action)
14. Jenny **<u>wondered</u>** about her future career (Mental Action)

15. I **<u>am</u>** who I **<u>am</u>**. (Linking Verbs)

Worksheet 1.10: Transitive and Intransitive Verbs

1. Alessia's arm <u>itched</u>. (Intransitive)
2. Simon **<u>folded</u>** his clothes. (**Transitive**)
3. Peter **<u>apologized</u>** to his sister. (**Transitive**)
4. Carrie <u>slept</u>. (Intransitive)
5. Lilly **<u>painted</u>** the wall purple. (**Transitive**)
6. The ladybug **<u>jumped</u>** onto the windowsill. (**Intransitive**)
7. Susie the moth **<u>flew</u>** over the flowers. (**Intransitive**)
8. Perry the penguin **<u>protected</u>** his eggs. (**Transitive**)
9. Hilly's feet <u>ached</u>. (Intransitive)
10. Roger <u>laughed</u> jubilantly. (Intransitive)
11. Celicia **<u>told</u>** her mom a story. (**Transitive**)
12. Victoria's questions **<u>remained</u>**. (**Intransitive**)
13. Cruella **<u>wore</u>** her lavish coat. (**Transitive**)
14. The dog **<u>smiled</u>** at her owner. (**Transitive**)
15. Villains are always **<u>stopped</u>**. (**Intransitive**)

Worksheet 1.11: Active and Passive Verbs

1. Silvia **<u>washed</u>** her dad's car. (**Active**)
2. The house **<u>was painted</u>** in two days. (**Passive**)
3. Jessica **<u>talked</u>** to her friend on the phone. (**Active**)
4. The plate **<u>was broken</u>** by Janet. (**Passive**)
5. Ricky **<u>stoked</u>** the flames in the hearth. (**Active**)
6. Karen **<u>hugged</u>** her mother. (**Active**)
7. Jordan **<u>was given</u>** a blue sweater for her birthday. (**Passive**)
8. Many people **<u>live</u>** in the city. (**Active**)
9. The city **<u>is inhabited</u>** by many people.

(Passive)

10. The teacher <u>**was surprised**</u> by her student's behavior. **(Passive)**
11. Jillian's father <u>**changed**</u> the oil in her car. **(Active)**
12. Tabitha <u>**asked**</u> her mom a question. **(Active)**
13. The party <u>**was**</u> abruptly <u>**ended**</u> by its host. **(Passive)**
14. Susie the caterpillar <u>**was catapulted**</u> from the branch. **(Passive)**
15. Grant <u>**asked**</u> his father for permission to go on the trip. **(Active)**

Worksheet 1.12: Verb Tense

1. Sandra <u>**went**</u> to the market. (Past)
2. David <u>**will have completed**</u> his paper by Tuesday. (Future Perfect)
3. Mark <u>**has been doing**</u> many chores around the house. (Present Perfect)
4. The car <u>**will go**</u> to the shop tomorrow. (Future)
5. Everyone <u>**is dancing**</u> at the party. (Present)
6. Maria <u>**had hoped**</u> to see her friend at the carnival. (Past Perfect)
7. Edward <u>**visited**</u> the castle. (Past)
8. Susan <u>**will have made**</u> 6 pies for the bake sale. (Future Perfect)
9. Carrie the chipmunk <u>**has been stashing**</u> many acorns. (Present Perfect)
10. The comedian <u>**is joking**</u> around. (Present)
11. William <u>**had expected**</u> more from the luncheon. (Past Perfect).
12. Tracy <u>**will have written**</u> 20 letters to her friend. (Future Perfect)
13. The Great Depression <u>**was**</u> a difficult time. (Past)
14. I <u>**am**</u> happy. (Present)
15. The CEO <u>**gave**</u> her address to the company. (Past)

Worksheet 1.13: Adjectives and Adverbs

Adjectives are underlined and adverbs are bolded

1. Jake peered **timidly** around the corner.
2. Scarlett **softly** pet the <u>fluffy</u> cat.
3. Marie drank the <u>cool</u> water **slowly**.
4. After being in the <u>hot</u> sun for hours, Bob was **definitely** ready for a <u>cold</u> shower!
5. Liam admired the <u>turquoise</u> shoes, but knew he had <u>very little</u> money.
6. *Fahrenheit 451* is an <u>excellent</u> book and I would **highly** recommend it.
7. The twins look **frighteningly** similar.
8. The <u>fancy</u> motel was **oddly** inexpensive.
9. The girl laughed **menacingly** at the <u>little</u> boy..
10. Everyone **politely** complimented Sarah's <u>new</u> apartment.
11. The <u>shy</u> boy made a friend, much to his mother's relief.
12. Nobody understood the <u>quirky blonde</u> girl.

Worksheet 1.14: What Adverbs Modify

1. Martha spoke <u>**very quickly**</u>. (M.Adv, M. Verb.)
2. Jenny's hands were <u>**expectedly**</u> wrinkled. (M Adj.)
3. The stewardess handed out the snacks <u>**kindly**</u>. (M Verb)
4. The outcome was <u>**inexplicably**</u> positive. (M Adj.)
5. Everyone says that Candace runs <u>**quite awkwardly**</u>. (M Adv., M. Verb)
6. Noah built his house <u>**carefully**</u>. (M Verb)
7. Sandra's sweet mother loved her <u>**tenderly**</u>. (M Verb)
8. The party was <u>**exceptionally**</u> quiet. (M Adj.)
9. Construction workers repaved the highway <u>**very slowly**</u>. (M Adv., M. Verb)
10. Jakob's vacation felt <u>**strangely**</u> like a new life. (Adv. M Verb)

11. The new car was **too** expensive for the college student. (M Adj.)
12. People often think **too simply**. (M Adv., M. Verb)

Worksheet 1.15: Articles

1. A dog is a loyal animal.
2. Cats are the best animals, though.
3. The platypus is an egg-laying mammal.
4. Alaska is the biggest state in the U.S.
5. Cheryl is an A+ student.
6. Rhode Island is a very small state.
7. Alex is getting an updo at the salon.
8. Music is often a catalyst for change.

Worksheet 1.16: Prepositional Phrases
1. Kary told her mom **about the party**.
2. The goldfish swam **around the tank**.
3. **Across the shore**, the sun shone brightly.
4. We may never know what happened **after she left**.
5. The tourists climbed **aboard the cruise ship**.
6. The two remained friends **through it all**.
7. Snowball the cat played **with her toy mouse**.
8. Marcos decided to pour time **into the new project**.
9. **Behind closed doors**, one finds only dead ends.
10. **During the play**, one actress sprained her ankle.
11. Cats tend to not like people, **except their owners**.
12. Jake waited **until the car arrived** to say goodbye.

Worksheet 1.17: Conjunctions

1. You must have **either** a permission slip **or** a parent's verbal approval to go on the trip. (Correlative)
2. Would you like tea with breakfast **or** would you prefer juice? (Coordinating)
3. We will go to the park **since** the sun is out. (Subordinating)
4. James and Susie wanted to play, **but** their parents asked them to do chores. (Coordinating)
5. Leah wanted **not only** her entire family at her party, **but also** all of her friends. (Correlative)
6. Tatyanna couldn't decide between using the orange crayon **and** using the green one. (Coordinating)
7. **Because** they delayed lunch, Noah was not able to go home to eat. (Subordinating)
8. **Since** everyone was already gone, the janitor decided to listen to music while he cleaned. (Subordinating)
9. Money doesn't bring **either** happiness **or** satisfaction. (Correlative)
10. I would love to go outside, **yet** it is raining quite hard,. (Coordinating)

Worksheet 1.18: Interjections and Appositives

1. Mason, **the quietist manager**, is out for lunch. (Appositive)
2. **Oh my**, that is quite unfortunate! (Interjection)
3. Susie said, "**Yuck**!" when she opened the garbage can. (Interjection)
4. Hortense, **the understanding landlord**, extended our lease. (Appositive)
5. **Goodness** Irsula, how many hours did it take to complete that recipe? (Interjection)
6. **The funniest girl at the table**, Clarisse, made yet another killer joke. (Appositive)
7. Fernanda, **the wisest woman in the room**, gave advice to the new mother. (Appositive)
8. **Oi**, that is one big mess! (Interjection)
9. **Oh my goodness**, will this change everything? (Interjection)
10. The intern, **a young boy from Scotland**, had a passion for the trade.

(Appositive)

11. **My stars**, the opportunity to be an actress is here at last! (Interjection)

12. Sun, **the CEO of the company**, is known for responding to questions with a resounding, "**Ugh!**" (Appositive, Interjection)

Unit 1 Test
Answers will vary.

Unit 2

Worksheet 2.1: Subjects and Predicates

The complete subject is underlined and the simple subject is emboldened.

1. The <u>young, intelligent **girl**</u> dreamed of becoming a scientist.
2. A <u>kind, helpful young **man**</u> helped an elderly woman with her groceries.
3. **Sofia**, a software developer, created a new app.
4. <u>Direct, honest **Darnell**</u> gave excellent feedback to his employee.
5. **Olgä** asked her brother to play with her.
6. The <u>patient **mother**</u> made a second attempt at teaching her child.

The complete predicate is underlined and the simple predicate is emboldened.

7. Hakan <u>**was** very **nervous**</u> about his solo.
8. Breonna <u>**has been working**</u> exceptionally hard.
9. The band <u>**was playing**</u> quite loudly.
10. The CEO <u>**spilled**</u> her burning coffee.
11. Everybody <u>**was** still **doing**</u> the right thing afterwards.
12. The cows <u>**had been** fervently **crying**</u> all night.

Worksheet 2.2: Direct and Indirect Objects

The direct objects are underlined, and the indirect objects are bolded.

1. Cordelia handed **Jamal** the <u>can opener</u>.
2. Phil opened the <u>can</u>.
3. Larissa told <u>Shay</u> that she was upset.
4. The milkman handed the <u>carton</u> to the boy.
5. Noah placed the <u>spoon</u> into the bowl.
6. The events that occurred helped <u>Stacey</u> find a new sense of hope.
7. After Liu gave her **mom** an <u>apology</u>, she felt much better.
8. Kindness creates <u>love</u>.
9. Cars help <u>people</u> go fast.
10. The butler gave his **employer** a <u>two-week notice</u>.
11. Shu-Ling braided her <u>hair</u>.
12. Tanisha drove her <u>car</u> to the mechanic.

Worksheet 2.3: Independent, Dependent, & Relative Clauses

1. The branch fell <u>where the children had been playing</u>. (Relative)
2. <u>Although Laila tried</u>, she could not convince her grandmother. (Dependent)
3. The mouse ate the cheese. (Independent)
4. While an attempt was made, <u>nothing could be done</u>. (Independent)
5. The cat <u>that chased away the mice</u> is named Fluffy. (Relative)
6. The friend <u>who Olgä had loved</u> remained present. (Relative)
7. <u>The water dripped</u> through the awning. (Independent)
8. We don't have enough time to go to the carnival <u>even though you are done with your homework</u>. (Dependent)
9. Will you tell me <u>when the cows come home</u>? (Dependent)
10. Everyone wants what they do not have but <u>this will make them unhappy</u>. (Independent)
11. Thank you for coming. (Independent)
12. The children, <u>when they were</u>

<u>questioned</u>, answered honestly.
(Relative)

Worksheet 2.4: Types of Sentences

1. While he did apologize, his tone was not sincere, and he was looking at the ground the whole time. (Compound-Complex)
2. I had to run to the store to make it before it closed. (Complex)
3. When we went to the movies the other day, we really enjoyed the film. (Complex)
4. The siblings hugged each other. (Simple)
5. He should stay here, yet he has decided to go there. (Compound)
6. Although we stayed on schedule the entire trip, we are all quite exhausted, and we didn't get the experience we were hoping for. (Compound-Complex)
7. Pierre went to see his family. (Simple)
8. Natalia was going to school for journalism, but now she is going for architecture. (Compound)
9. Although she made a careful outline, Jazz decided to draw all over the page. (Complex)
10. LaShawn is moving to New York, for he has been offered a job there. (Compound)
11. Love is the answer. (Simple)
12. I was initially worried about the interview, but the interviewer was really friendly and I was wearing my favorite outfit. (Compound-Complex)

Worksheet 2.5: Kinds of Sentences

1. What an excellent vacation! (Exclamatory)
2. What city is your new friend from? (Interrogative)
3. I enjoy classical music. (Declarative)
4. Get some fresh tea from the cupboard. (Imperative)
5. I wish today was Friday. (Declarative)

6. I can't wait to get there! (Exclamatory)
7. I couldn't be more touched! (Exclamatory)
8. Do you like the gift I gave you for your birthday? (Interrogative)
9. Don't be impolite. (Imperative)
10. Clean your room before we leave this afternoon. (Imperative)
11. Have you ever been to London? (Interrogative)
12. I have been to London. (Declarative)

Worksheet 2.6: Sentence Summary

- The bed had been jumped on by the children. (Declarative, passive, past perfect)
- Susie will have been to all 50 states by the end of the year. (Declarative, active, future perfect)
- Will anyone tell me what is going on? (Interrogative, active, future)
- Leave now so that you can make it back in time. (Imperative, active, present)
- I can't believe you had been planning this surprise party the whole time! (Exclamatory, active, past perfect)
- How is anyone being deceived? (Interrogative, passive, present)
- Make sure that the cake has been picked up by noon. (Imperative, passive, future perfect)
- I wanted to go, but I couldn't. (Declarative, active, past)
- The bird will be startled at the slightest noise. (Declarative, passive, future)
- May I go play with the other children? (Interrogative, active, present)

Unit 2 Test
Answers will vary

Unit 3

Worksheet 3.1: Identifying Fragments

1. Without a goodbye. (F)
2. She went to the store. (NF)

3. The cat from the shelter. (F)
4. Employees in the factory. (F)
5. All that flour in the bowl. (F)
6. People go to work. (NF)
7. Everyone who resides in the neighborhood. (F)
8. The lazy dogs napped. (NF)
9. Everyone says he is kind. (NF)
10. The fox in the hen house. (F)

Worksheet 3.2: Correcting Fragments
Answers will vary.

Worksheet 3.3: Identify Run-ons and Comma Splices
1. I built the house, she paved the driveway. (CS)
2. We bought the farm, they sold it to us. (CS)
3. We moved to the farm on Sunday our neighbors brought us an apple pie on Monday. (RO)
4. She braided my hair, my sister curled hers. (CS)
5. I opened the barn on Monday rats ran out a calf bleated. (RO)
6. When we left the city I was sad I am happier at the farm though. (RO)
7. My parents are out of town my sister and I are staying with our grandparents. (RO)
8. They shrieked, we cried. (CS)
9. I jumped, he remained still. (CS)
10. Every time I milk the cows they bleat chickens don't like the noise so they cluck angrily. (RO)

Worksheet 3.4: Correcting Run-ons and Comma Splices
Answers will vary

Worksheet 3.5: Rambling/Wordy Sentences
Answers will vary.

1. We went to the store, but I forgot my mask, and when I went back to the car to check for it, I realized that I left it at home. (R/W)
2. The car hurdled down the road at an alarming speed, leaving onlookers in awe. (NOT R/W)
3. Generation X chose to settle down and have families, but millennials have had children at much lower rates, and Generation Z is predicted to produce even fewer children in adulthood. (R/W)
4. Going on road trips is a lot of fun and can be an important bonding experience, but there are many dangers of cross country trips such as flat tires, mechanical issues, and highway hypnosis. (R/W)
5. Telling the truth is difficult, but lying is even harder. (NOT R/W)
6. The chipmunk accused a squirrel of stealing her acorn, but it was actually a neighboring deer who was responsible for the missing acorn because she took it that morning when the chipmunk was busy. (R/W)
7. Some parts of the country are mountainous or near the ocean, while other parts are flat and barren. (NOT R/W)
8. The earlier one begins to save money, the earlier they can retire, unless the economy is not doing well, in which case they might have to save money over a longer period of time. (R/W)

Worksheet 3.6: Unclear Pronoun References

Answers will vary. The pronoun that needs to be adjusted is marked below,

1. The dog and the cat sat side by side until **she** had to leave.
2. If you arrive after the launch time, **they** won't allow you on the boat..
3. Sabina and LaToya are spending the day together, but **she** has to stop by her house first.
4. Because the companies will be held

accountable, **you** should keep your books properly.

5. Christine enjoyed the work, but Casey felt that **she** was underpaid.
6. Jacob got a B+ and Caleb got an A-, but **he** felt that his grade was not good enough.
7. The data showed a drop in sales and an increase in labor, but **this** was not reflected in the report.
8. The school announced that **they** will be having a picnic next week.
9. Because mental health is important, **you** should remember to check in with yourself frequently.
10. Ronald was loud and did not apologize, **which** was frustrating.

Worksheet 3.7: Subject-Verb Agreement

- Sasha (**is** / are) a fluffy gray dog.
- Many people at the party (**think** / thinks) the music is enjoyable.
- The Hankins (was / **were**) a happy family.
- Sugar (rot / **rots**) your teeth in excess.
- Raindrops (is / **are**) cool and refreshing.
- Rhea and Midori (**like** / likes) watching TV together.
- Everyone at the play (delight / **delights**) in the performance.
- The tablet or the paper (**is** / are) in the drawer.
- My mom, as well as all us children, (**has** / have) curly hair.
- The boy with all the action figures (bring / **brings**) his toys to share.

Worksheet 3.8: Misplaced and Dangling Modifiers

Answers will vary.

Worksheet 3.9: Parallelism
Answers will vary.

Unit 3 Test

It are not uncommon for two people to gaze upon the same picture but see it in completely unique ways, and this is the case with Hamlet and Willy because it cannot be argued that either of them made good choices. (**Rambling/Wordy, Comma Splice, Subject/Verb Agreement**) They fail to see the hurt they are causing doing whatever they want (**Misplaced Modifier**). Both of their goals contribute to much personal suffering and hurt those around them too. The difference between these two men (**Fragment**). Hamlet thinks through his plans and considers their impact every time, Willy make choices without considering their effect on others (**Comma Splice, Subject/Verb Agreement**). Both men who made mistakes (**Fragment**). They both face tough circumstances, Hamlet chooses to channel grief into action, Willy refuses to accept the consequences of his actions (**Run-On, Comma Splice, Unclear Pronoun Reference**).

In walking through their lives and mental processes, it becomes quite clear that both men are control by the events that the plays are based around (**SVA**). For Hamlet it are the deception of his father at the hands of his uncle and his mother's swift friendship to him (**UCP, SVA**). Because he cannot accept the new state of his life (**FR**). Hamlet starts down a path of vengeance and anger from which he knows that he cannot return, but a rational man would not take such foolish and dangerous actions that could only end in tragedy for himself and those around him (**RO**). Hamlet was blinded by his grief, Willy are a man who regrets his past actions and feels as if he has fallen short of his goals (**CS, SVA**). Willy cannot accept his mistakes and appreciate the good things that his choices have brought, which is evidenced by his delusional state of mind and deflective speech, for instance, Willy's older son Biff catch him in the midst of a lie (**RO, SVA**). Instead of fessing up to his lie, Willy simply become angry at Biff for running away in tears (**SVA**). Biff goes downhill after this, but Willy refuses to recognize his part in it. As Biff returns home a decade later, Willy's delusions worsen severely. He allows his fantasy of success to go too far, is unstable, and was not being realistic (**Parallelism**). Living in denial, his life fell apart (**DGLP**). A more stable person would have simply made incremental lifestyle changes to accommodate their goal, Willy is all about instant gratification and it holds him back (**CS**). Hamlet and Willy have similar fates, but he gets to them through different means (**UCP**).

Unit 4

Worksheet 4.1: Lists

Note: the word before the comma addition is bolded, to make the correction easier to see.

1. Lauren wrote papers about her **parents,** the first man to walk on the **moon,** and a famous actress.
2. Before he went to school, he got **dressed,** fixed his **hair,** and ate breakfast.
3. I went walking with my best **friend,** my **dog,** and my little sister.
4. On my birthday, I want to go for a **hike,** eat lots of **cake,** and have a sleepover with my friends.
5. My dad asked me to take care of my **brothers,** the **dog,** and the cat while he is away.
6. I eat **breakfast, lunch,** and dinner every day.
7. Jenny invited her three **cousins, Susan,** and Joe to the party.
8. Rachel likes **baking,** collecting **coins,** and riding horses.

Worksheet 4.2: Coordinating Conjunctions

Answers may vary slightly.

1. I went to the store, and my sister asked me to pick up avocados.
2. She left the country, but she never forgot where she came from.
3. True apologies are difficult, for they require genuine remorse.
4. We could go rollerskating, or we could go ice skating.
5. My parents took me to a theme park, and then they bought me dinner.
6. My older brother is 18, and my younger brother is 12.
7. We can't go to the beach, nor can we go to the mountains.
8. The resort is quite expensive, yet I still desire to go.

Worksheet 4.3: Dependent Clauses

Note: the word before the comma addition is bolded, to make the correction easier to see.

1. Although she never expected **it,** Lana became a movie star.
2. Before he left for **work,** Steve helped his kids with their homework.
3. Since Sarah said **yes,** Beth put her to work right away.
4. I watered all the plants since it hasn't rained in three days. (no comma needed)
5. Although James had not expected **it,** the job opportunity prompted him to move to San Francisco.
6. Unlike her old **friends,** Jane felt comfortable with her new friends.
7. Riddhi wanted to surprise her husband with a trip although she knew it would be tricky. (no comma needed)
8. Since the party was **busy,** Alex chose to bring everyone into the backyard.
9. Although the airplane had not even taken **off,** several passengers were becoming nervous.
10. While it had not been **planned,** the trip to the waterpark was quite fun.

Worksheet 4.4: Transition Phrases

Note: the word before the comma addition is bolded, to make the correction easier to see.

1. **Tom**, **however,** didn't find the music to his liking.
2. In **summary,** it is important that we all wash our hands.
3. She was late **again,** of course.
4. In the first **place,** the sloppiness of my roommate is rather disrespectful.
5. **Next,** we will marinate the meat for the barbeque tomorrow.
6. The most important **thing, then,** is to make sure your kids know you love them.
7. My **father, meanwhile,** always falls asleep three-quarters of the way through the movie.
8. **Otherwise,** it will be impossible to find our keys again.
9. When Ruby gave me her necklace to wear, I knew she trusted **me,** finally.
10. **Besides,** there are lots of times when we have to work hard.

Worksheet 4.5: Interjections and Appositives
Note: the word before the comma addition is bolded, to make the correction easier to see.

1. **Wow,** the garbage smells really bad.
2. **Julia,** our **babysitte**r, makes great peanut butter cookies.
3. **Eugene,** I would like you to take the dog for a walk.
4. I want to play with the green **car,** not the purple **one,** when Timmy comes over this evening.
5. I burned my finger yesterday, **and, ouch,** it hurts!
6. I just made a lasagna for **Maria,** our neighbor.
7. Oh **no,** it's starting to rain!
8. You are supposed to use **basil,** not **oregano,** in that recipe
9. My two **brothers,** Thomas and **Dean,** helped us move into our new house
10. **Gee,** it's a long walk to get to the waterfall.

Worksheet 4.6: Addresses and Dates
Note: the word before the comma addition is bolded, to make the correction easier to see.

1. Maya was born on January **12,** 1999.
2. On our road trip, we stopped at 7477 Hubbard **Avenue, Middleton,** Wisconsin 53562.
3. Nathan is coming to visit us in June 2021. (no comma)
4. The wedding will take place on September **7, 2020,** at the event center.
5. Trent's family lived at 855 Visionary **Trail, Golden,** Colorado **80401,** before they moved away.
6. The date of December **7,** 1941 is a "day that will live in infamy."
7. I entered 114 North Main **Street, Roswell,** New Mexico **88203,** into my navigation system.
8. We will celebrate Mildred's birthday in April 2021. (no comma)

Unit 4 Test

Part 1
Note: the word before the comma addition is bolded, to make the correction easier to see.

I walked to my Aunt Sally's house on May **21, 1998,** 6 weeks before my 12th birthday. Before I **arrived,** she made sure to have all of my favorite snacks and games ready. Her home was a lovely old house with ivy growing on the front **wall,** sitting proudly at 2323 Main **Street, Brooklyn,** New York 10001. **Gee,** it was a lovely house! As soon as I walked **in,** the aroma of fresh baked cookies met my nostrils sweetly and I heard my aunt humming quietly in the kitchen. When I entered the **kitchen,** she gave me a big hug and sat me down at the table for cookies and games. I won at **Monopoly,** but she beat me soundly at spades. We also played **chess, Jenga,** and checkers. It was an amazing day. This particular **aunt,** who lived with my family when I was a **baby,** was my favorite aunt growing up.

Sentences: Answer will vary

Unit 5

Worksheet 5.1: Capitalization

- I have a dentist's appointment on **W**ednesday afternoon.
- My grandparents' names are Lucas and **P**atricia.
- **T**hey went to the grocery store yesterday.
- My history class is taking a field trip to **P**hiladelphia in **A**ugust.
- In the show that **I** watch, the country is led by **P**resident **R**obertson.
- I decided to drive **e**ast on my road trip.
- I bought the perfect gift for **M**om this **C**hristmas.
- Julie and **I** are having lunch sometime this **s**ummer.
- My birthday is in **J**uly.
- The bill was just signed by **G**overnor **B**utterfield.
- This **w**inter, my **d**ad and **I** are traveling to **M**aine.
- My friend **B**obby lives **s**outh of me.

Worksheet 5.2: Titles

Note: when using proper punctuation for books, movies, and plays, italicizing and underlining are considered to both be acceptable--you should italicize when using a computer, but underlining is acceptable when using a typewriter or handwriting.

1. In the play *The Death of a Salesman,* Willie Lowman has to come to terms with mistakes he made in his life.
2. One of my favorite books is *Anne of Green Gables* because the main character is not perfect and is so relatable.
3. In the 1980s, many celebrities helped raise money by participating in the recording of the song "We Are the World."
4. Edgar Allen Poe's short story "The Tell-tale Heart" is an example of a story told by an unreliable narrator.
5. As a child, I would watch and rewatch *The Princess Bride* because it was such a good movie.
6. The poem "I, Too, Sing America" is by Langston Hughes.
7. The song "Yellow" is my favorite track on Coldplay's album *Parachutes.*
8. Have you seen the remake of the Disney movie *The Lion King*?

Worksheet 5.3: Punctuating with Variety
Answers will vary.

Worksheet 5.4: Semicolons

- I am so happy that I finally won a prize; I have been training for months.
- I have cousins in Atlanta, Georgia; Bangor, Maine; and Detroit, Michigan.
- I lived in Switzerland for 20 years; it was an incredible experience.
- My mom makes baklava when I come home; she makes it better than anyone else.
- The dog barked at the cat; they don't get along.
- Susie the caterpillar climbed up the fence; she does it every Sunday,
- Läslow the marmot scampered away; the hikers scared her.
- Mice often burrow in small spaces; they hide well.

Worksheet 5.5: Apostrophes

1. The familys cat hissed. (**family's**)
2. Her moms new blouse was ripped. (**mom's**)
3. The Gildans home was blown away in the tornado. (**Gildan's**)

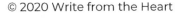

4. Janes house is blue. **(Jane's)**
5. The car ran over roberts foot. **(Robert's)**

6. The twins **have not** been to the theme park. **(Haven't)**
7. Jake would not tell a lie. (Wouldn't)
8. Susan **will not** be at the party. **(Won't)**
9. **You are** my best friend. **(You're)**
10. It is Sunday. (It's)

Worksheet 5.6: Punctuation and Sentence Summary
Answers will vary.

Unit 5 Test
Answers will vary.

Unit 6

Worksheet 6.1: Fragments

Answers will vary. Here is one possibility:

Herbology is the study of plants. Many folks are involved with herbology as a hobby. Being an herbalist requires a deep love for plants. Most herbologists understand various uses and ways to care for plants. While many folks are searching for healthier and more natural ways of living, herbology is becoming more and more prominent.

Worksheet 6.2: Run-ons and Comma Splices

Answers will vary. Here is one possibility:

The Mainstreet Dog Park is a very nice place. **A lot of people in town enjoy visiting with their dogs.** I enjoy the shaded seating and multiple watering spots. My dog, Lucky, a feisty chocolate lab, became friends with another dog, Fido. **They played together for hours on our first visit and even longer the second visit.** Frank, Fido's owner, is a nice guy, he lives a few blocks away. **His apartment is right around the corner from my favorite ice cream place.** Going to the dog park is a regular event for Lucky and me. **We both love a lot of things it offers and intend to keep going for the rest of the summer.**

Worksheet 6.3: Rambling and Wordy Sentences

Answers will vary. Here is one possibility:

Teaching is a challenging profession, and it requires much of those who work in it and oftentimes requires big trade-offs. The trade-offs are personal, financial, and professional. In other careers, there are numerous opportunities to socialize throughout the day. Teaching, especially in lower elementary, rarely gives you the time to chat with coworkers. It is no secret that teaching is also an underpaid profession. Teachers frequently use their own funds to purchase needed supplies such as crayons, pencils, kleenex, markers, and other craft supplies. Finally, teaching is a taxing profession. The amount of work and long hours limit opportunities to pursue further schooling and professional development. These challenges are large and difficult. The challenges of teaching do not diminish the many benefits and joys that come with teaching as a profession.

Worksheet 6.4: Unclear Pronouns

Answers will vary. Here is one possibility:

To Kill a Mockingbird by Harper Lee is considered by some to be an important and essential book. Across the country, many students read the book in their classrooms and engage in conversations around the subject matter. **The book** leads to important discussions on race, justice, and involvement in the community. Teachers often craft various lessons around the book, which helps **students** delve deeper into the content. **Teachers** frequently speak of the lasting impact **the book** has in the classrooms. **For many,** *To Kill a Mockingbird* **is an important text to**

complete and learn from. The impact of this book is what sets the text apart from many other books read throughout schools in this country.

Worksheet 6.5 Subject-Verb Agreement
My mother, Taraji, **celebrates** Kwanza every December. It is an important holiday for her and our family. Kwanza is focused on seven principles, and they **are**: Umoja, Kujichagulia, Ujima, Ujamaa, Nia, Kuumba, Imani. Each of these principles **is** celebrated one a day, for all seven days of the holiday's season. These principles **translate** to mean: unity, self-determination, collective work, cooperative economics, purpose, creativity, and faith. Maulana Karenga, the creator of the Holiday, wanted a holiday for African Americans that was separate from Christmas and provided a space solely for the African-American community to celebrate and come together. My mother **believes** in that vision and **continues** the tradition in our family. She **hopes** I do the same with my future family.

Worksheet 6.5: Misplaced and Dangling Modifiers

Answers will vary. Here is one possibility:

There are many types of cats in this world. My favorite breed is the Russian Blue. Russian Blues are known for silky blue-ish fur and yellow eyes. I first saw a Russian Blue, while I was walking past a local bookstore. The cat actually caught my attention because of its color and size. With bulky fur, the cat makes me want to pet one.. Another aspect of this breed is them being hypoallergenic, which rarely cause flare-ups for folks allergic to cats. Russian Blues are both beautiful and friendly, making them a great option for a pet.

Worksheet 6.7: Parallelism

I love going to the movies. The local movie theater has everything you could want: **exciting movies, satisfying food, refreshing air conditioning, and relaxing seats**. During the summer it is the most popular spot to be. Oftentimes you can see many friends going together. They might **be looking for a fun activity that gets them out of the heat or looking to catch the newest film**. Either way, it is the place to be. The local theater offers plenty of fun and amenities to the community.

Worksheet 6.8: Commas

Note: the word before the comma addition is bolded, to make the correction easier to see.

John **Locke,** a philosopher in the **1600's,** lived in England during a troubled time. Many people who disagreed with the monarchy's free reign were arrested and sometimes killed. Because of his ideas that rulers of a country have limited **power,** Locke was forced to flee England to save his life. Years **later,** Locke was finally free to write down his ideas when King William and Queen Mary initiated a constitutional monarchy. A constitutional monarchy is a monarchy where the king has to obey rules laid down by **Parliament,** an elected legislature. This was different from the former **monarchy,** where the monarch had no accountability. (6)

John Locke's ideas influenced other **countries,** like America and France. The American Revolution began in the **1770's,** sparked by the king of **England,** King George **III,** and his tyranny towards America. After the Revolutionary **War,** Locke's ideas were used as the foundation of the American Constitution. After America broke away from **England,** the **French,** who had helped America fight during the **revolution,** saw the application and benefits of Locke's ideas in the colonies. After returning from the war in the **colonies,** the French became more and more discontent with the absolute monarch that ruled their country. The French revolted and successfully got rid of their king. (9)

Worksheet 6.9: Essay Editing 1
The errors are marked as follows:
Frag=Fragment, CS=Comma Splice, RO= Run-on, SVA=Subject-verb agreement, MDM=Misplaced or dangling modifier, RW=rambling or wordy sentences, Par=Parallelism error. Comma errors have the word immediately before the comma bolded.

Animal Crossing: New Horizons and Its Popularity
Video games has become increasingly more and more popular as time goes on.**(SVA)** There are countless types of games, from platforming games to role-playing games. Many folks who play them have their own specific tastes.**(UCP)** **Occasionally,** a video game will come around at the right time and pick-up a lot of fans, folks that previously did not play that sort of game. **(CS)** That is what occurred on the launch date of *Animal Crossing: New Horizons*. A video game that became a huge piece of pop culture and a worldwide phenomenon.**(Frag)** (5)
The Animal Crossing series has a lengthy history. The first version was released in Japan. Right before the launch of the Nintendo Gamecube. **(Frag)** After that first version was **released**, it steadily picked up fans and released new versions on a regular basis. The concept of the game is simple you are placed in a small village with animal neighbors and can engage in various activities like fishing and bug-catching. **(RO)** For **many**, this game is considered peaceful and relaxing and offers a break from other louder and more action-packed video games. (4)
With every new release of Animal Crossing, the developers offer new features and gameplay for players to engage with because it's fun and everyone seems to like it, so they keep putting them out. **(RW)** Although it had a dedicated group of fans, it never became as mainstream as other Nintendo titles like the Pokemon **series**, Legend of Zelda **games**, or Mario games. It would change in 2020. **(UCP)** In late **2019,** Nintendo announced an upcoming release of the newest Animal Crossing game, *New Horizons*. It was met with celebration by its fanbase and was eagerly awaited. The newest version was released on March **20, 2020,** which coincided with a sudden increase in stay-at-home orders and social distancing rules related to the international COVID-19 outbreak.(7)
This caused a sharp uptick in sales and popularity. **(UCP)** Many folks found the game's relaxed gameplay a perfect respite from increasingly what was becoming a more difficult and scarier world. **(MDM)** Social media was flooded with images of folks holding online graduation ceremonies, weddings, recreating popular game shows, and talk shows.**(Par)** The excitement was only further increased as more of the game's features were discovered such as **terra-forming**, a landscaping feature that allows for full customization. The game's popularity began to draw folks that traditionally played other genres of video games or was not video game players prior to the release. **(SVA)** (5)
Animal Crossing: New Horizons are a great example of a video game gaining mass popularity. **(SVA)** Not only did the game have a solid fanbase prior to its **launch**, but it also picked up new fans and new gamers due to world events. The game offered a perfect space to play, create, and relax while offering opportunities to interact digitally with friends while maintaining social distancing because it was hard not to see friends and family. **(RW)** For these reasons *Animal Crossing: New Horizons* will most likely maintain its status in pop culture and be a video game that many will remember. For a long time. **(Frag)** (4)
Worksheet 6.10: Essay Editing 2
The errors are marked as follows:
Frag=Fragment, CS=Comma Splice, RO= Run-on, SVA=Subject-verb agreement, MDM=Misplaced or dangling modifier, RW=rambling or wordy sentences, Par=Parallelism error. Comma errors have the word immediately before the comma bolded.

Worksheet 6.10: Essay Editing 2
The errors are marked as follows:
Frag=Fragment, CS=Comma Splice, RO= Run-on, SVA=Subject-verb agreement, MDM=Misplaced or dangling modifier, RW=rambling or wordy sentences. Comma errors have the word immediately before the comma bolded.

Catherine Morland, the main character in Jane Austen's novel <u>Northanger Abbey</u>, **(or italicize)** is forced to endure numerous harsh trials throughout her story. Although this is hard for **her**, it results in a maturity beyond her years in one scenario she must share quarters with a suspected murderer.**(RO)** Or worse. **(Frag)** In another, the person she <u>only</u> **(goes in front of "person")** loves catches her in a foolish act. And at one point, she must use all her mental and physical strength to do something that brings displeasure to her brother and dearest friends. It seems that everything she **does**, anything she **thinks**, and all the people she interacts with brings harm upon her or a loved one. Is Austen kind enough to let her main character live a happy ending? The answer to this question is played out wonderfully in *Northanger Abbey*, intermingled with inspiring gothic themes.

Jane Austen uses adventure and mystery as a prominent gothic element in her novel by creating a chilling suspense in the reader and it's all very unsettling and creepy. **(RW)** Such creepy adventures includes a visit to a large and ominous **abbey**, which is the main source of the intrigue. **(SVA)** General Tilney is the person who runs it, Catherine strays from the grounds of common sense and is tempted to suspect the <u>Generals</u> **General's** motives. **(CS)** But even more mysterious are the large locked chests Catherine discovers in her room. The foreboding hallway which leads to the door of the deceased Mrs. <u>Tilneys</u> **Tilney's** bedroom. **(Frag)** Imagining dark things, the ideas Catherine comes up earn her dire consequences. **(MDM)**

Another striking theme in the book <u>Northanger Abbey</u> **(or italicize)** is the study of the inner self. Catherine is posed with several opportunities to judge. Between true love and deceptive infatuation. **(Frag)** Even her closest friend **Isabella**, someone she would never have dreamed to be an outright **liar**, ends up lying to her face more than once. And Catherine herself is forced to decide whether to go on an outing with friends or wait for her stuffy hosts. The author ingeniously deals with the difficult situations which tear at Catherines **Catherine's** soul. If she makes a bad **decision**, her guilt will ruin the days that pass until she sets it straight.

Perhaps the most important element in Austen's novel is her own commentary on gothic novels of her time. **Nowadays**, it seems to be unacceptable for the author to openly comment on other people's tastes while the story is still in the middle of the action, but that is what Austen does and she gives her view on gothic novels and culture of her time. **(RW)** In several **places**, she exaggerate her own story in order to poke fun at the stupidity of other novels. **(SVA)** While slightly amusing, her spicy comments are helpful when you are looking for a better understanding of gothic literature of the 18th century. In **fact**, it seems that Jane <u>Austens</u> **Austen's** whole purpose when writing her story was to provide the world with an extensive knowledge of her opinions.

I recommend <u>Northanger Abbey</u> **(or italicize)** as an excellent gothic novel to read. It is full of stimulating **adventures**, emotional introspection of the human **heart** ,and wonderful opportunities to get a first-hand biased view on gothic literature.

Made in the USA
Monee, IL
01 August 2020